The Agony of the Promised Land

The Agony of the Promised Land

Joshua Levy

iUniverse, Inc.
New York Lincoln Shanghai

The Agony of the Promised Land

iUniverse, Inc.

For information address:
iUniverse, Inc.
2021 Pine Lake Road, Suite 100
Lincoln, NE 68512
www.iuniverse.com

ISBN: 0-595-32133-X

Printed in the United States of America

Contents

List of Maps . . . . *ix*

Preface . . . . *xi*

Chapter 1   THE PATRIARCHS AND THE PROMISED LAND 1

Chapter 2   THE KINGDOM OF ISRAEL AND THE FIRST TEMPLE 8

Chapter 3   THE DESTRUCTION OF THE SECOND TEMPLE 12

Chapter 4   JUDEA RENAMED 'PHILISTIA' 19

Chapter 5   THE DIASPORA 22

Chapter 6   MUHAMMAD AND ISLAM 33

Chapter 7   THE EXPANSION AND CONQUESTS OF ISLAM 41

Chapter 8   ANTI-SEMITISM AND ZIONISM 51

Chapter 9   ARABS AND JEWS IN PALESTINE 60

Chapter 10   ISRAEL'S WAR OF INDEPENDENCE 85

Chapter 11   THE SINAI CAMPAIGN 96

Chapter 12   THE SIX-DAY WAR 100

Chapter 13   YOM KIPPUR WAR 109

Chapter 14   FROM THE SIX-DAY WAR TO THE
OSLO AGREEMENT 114

Chapter 15   THE COLLAPSE OF THE OSLO
AGREEMENT 123

Chapter 16   THE AL-AQSA INTIFADA 130

Chapter 17   LEADERS AND CHILDREN IN THE
VIOLENCE 142

Chapter 18   INCITEMENT BY THE ARAB
COUNTRIES 150

Chapter 19   OPERATION 'DEFENSIVE SHIELD'
AND JENIN 156

Chapter 20   THE ROLE OF THE MEDIA IN THE
CONFLICT 161

Chapter 21   THE LEGALITY OF TARGETING
TERRORISTS 169

Chapter 22   THE MAIN OBSTACLES FOR
PEACE 174

Chapter 23   THE HOPE FOR PEACE 187

Chapter 24   CONCLUSION 198

Bibliography 201

Index 207

Acknowledgements

I want to thank my dear wife Judith for her support and immense help and patience during the writing of this book; Dr. Jeff Malka for reading the manuscript and for his helpful comments and suggestions; the Israeli Embassy in London for their important documented information; Sophie Youri for her help with the maps; and last but not least, my friends who encouraged me to write this book; in particular Geoffrey Galley who first inspired me to undertake this task.

List of Maps

MAP 1 UR, HARAN AND CANAAN 7

MAP 2 ISRAEL AND ITS ARAB NEIGHBOURS 81

MAP 3 - AREAS SEPARATED FROM PALESTINE AND 82
GIVEN TO EMIR ABDULLAH BY BRITAIN IN 1921
- AREAS SEPARATED FROM PALESTINE AND
GIVEN TO THE FRENCH MANDATE OF SYRIA IN
1923

MAP 4 THE PEEL'S PARTITION PLAN—1937 83

MAP 5 U.N PARTITION PLAN—1947 84

MAP 6 ISRAEL BETWEEN 1949 AND 1967 95

MAP 7 ISRAEL AFTER THE SIX-DAY WAR 108

MAP 8 ISRAEL AFTER THE PEACE ACCORD WITH 122
EGYPT

Preface

As in the case of Solomon's Judgment, two peoples are holding a tiny piece of land and each claiming it is theirs. The Palestinians say they have been on this land for hundreds of years, and the Israelis say they have been there for thousands of years and had a kingdom in this land for centuries, with Jerusalem as its capital. The Palestinians say: dig under any Jewish settlement and you will find the ruins of an Arab settlement. The Israelis retort: keep on digging and you will find the ruins of a Jewish settlement under it. But, unlike Solomon's case, a land can be divided, which seems to be the only possible solution to the conflict, and yet, the protagonists are as far as ever from reaching this obvious conclusion, and the bloodshed continues.

This book analyses the obstacles for peace and discusses the possibility of removing them and the chances for reconciliation. It starts with a concise history of the two peoples involved, the political and religious aspect of the conflict; the affinity of the Jews and Arabs to this land; their wars; continuous fighting with each other; futile attempts of compromise and the present ferocious Intifada and its reasons and aims. It also reveals the influence of other Arab countries on the conflict, and discusses the role of the media and the hope for peace.

In discussions with ordinary as well as intellectual people, lack of knowledge was found regarding the origin of the Israeli-

Arab conflict, its history and background. Some people of the press, who write or report on this subject, often show surprising ignorance. For example, in an article titled "It's all Aramaic to Mel" (in a November 2002 edition of a prominent and popular American magazine) regarding Mel Gibson's film about Jesus 'The Passion of the Christ', the magazine described Aramaic as *"a language spoken in ancient Palestine"*. A knowledgeable reader wrote to the magazine explaining that there was no 'Palestine' at the time of Jesus, but a Jewish state called Judea, and that Aramaic, which is closely related to Hebrew, was spoken in Judea and Israel centuries before the birth of Jesus. In fact, parts of the Old Testament, like 'Ezra' and 'Daniel' for example, were written in Aramaic. Also, the vast compilation of the Talmud, while it contains much material in Hebrew, its basic language is Aramaic. The magazine's response was even more spectacular: *"We appreciate the interest that prompted your response to our scoop item 'It's all Aramaic to Mel'. We state that Aramaic was spoken in ancient Palestine because Israel, as a nation, did not exist before 1948. It had been part of northern Palestine. We again thank you for your response. Sincerely—(signed) for the editors."* The level of ignorance in this reply is of course lamentable, to say the least.

In view of the above, and with encouragement of some of my close friends, I decided to write this book as a brief digest of the past and present of Israel, Palestine, Jews and Arabs, their religion and politics, and the sad and violent conflict between the two peoples. It is thought that such a simple and short volume would appeal to those readers who wish to gain an understanding of the whole history and the conflict in a nutshell. It is of course hoped that the reading of this book would whet their appetite for a deeper knowledge and encourage them to read more in detail about this long and fascinating history.

The book begins with the first Jewish Patriarchs in Canaan and continues to discuss, in a very concise mode, the Kingdoms of Judah and Israel, the Diaspora, the birth of Islam, the Arab and Muslim expansion and occupation of Palestine. It also discusses Zionism, Israel's wars with the Arabs and the September 2000 Intifada to date. It ends up with a discussion on the present situation, the obstacles for peace and suggests a beam of hope for peace.

In relating the story of the Patriarchs, I have relied on narrative and verses from the Old Testament. Religious readers will certainly read them in context of the Holy Bible; others may want to view them as a chronicle of those ancient fathers who first lit the star of monotheism in the dark skies of paganism and idolatry.

I think that knowledge of the facts in this book, as well as the historical background of the peoples involved and their affinity to the Land, are imperative to those who are interested in, or wish to understand, one of the most intricate and dangerous conflicts in the world today.

1

THE PATRIARCHS AND THE PROMISED LAND

The story of Israel started about four thousand years ago with an unusual man called Abram, and later Abraham. Abraham was unusual because he lived in a world of pagans and idolaters and yet believed in a single God. He left his homeland, at the ancient city of Ur, on the Euphrates River in Mesopotamia, about 160 miles North West of the Persian Gulf, to find another place where he can worship his God un-harassed. So, he arrived in Haran, in North-West Mesopotamia, between the two big rivers of the Tigris and the Euphrates, about 10 miles north of today's Syrian border, inside Turkey.

The Bible tells us that shortly after he had arrived there, God called upon him to leave his country and his kindred and go into the land of Canaan (present day Israel). *"Get out of thy country, and from thy kindred, and from thy father's house, unto a land that I shall shew thee"* said God to Abraham, and Abraham took Sarah his wife, and Lot his brother's son, and their substance that they had gathered, and the souls that they had gotten in Haran, and they went forth to go to the land of Canaan. When they arrived there, God promised Abraham all the land of Canaan for an everlasting possession, to him and to his seed after him. God also made a covenant with Abraham whereby every man and child of his household should be circumcised. The Hebrew word for covenant is 'brit', thus, 'brit' is not the circumcision itself, but the covenant to circumcise, and Abraham was the first Hebrew to fulfil this covenant with God.

Subsequently, Abraham became very rich in Canaan. He had flocks and herds and tents, and so did Lot, his nephew. The land became unable to bear them to dwell together, and Lot had to go eastward and settle in the plain of Jordan, where it was fertile and well watered, while Abraham came and dwelt in the plain of Mamre, which is in today's Hebron, and built there an altar unto the Lord. Abraham and Sarah had only one son, Isaac. The bible tells us that God tested Abraham's loyalty by ordering him to take his only young son, Isaac, whom he loved, and offer him as a sacrifice. Only when Abraham was about to slay Isaac with a machete as ordered, did God send a ram and Abraham offered it up for a burnt offering instead of his son, and was blessed by the Lord. This was also a lesson to Abraham and the Jews that offering of human sacrifice, as done by the idolaters, was wrong, and that God would not accept such offering.

Isaac grew up and took Rebecca, his second cousin, granddaughter of his uncle Nachor from Haran, as wife. Rebecca gave Isaac two sons, the younger of whom was Jacob, who won his father's blessing before his death by a trick, for Esau, his brother, was the firstborn and the one entitled to his father's blessing. Jacob thus became the third Hebrew patriarch, after Abraham and Isaac. The word 'Hebrew' is thought to stem from the name of the tribe that Abraham came from, but beside

Hebrews and Jews, the descendants of Abraham, Isaac and Jacob are also known as Israelites, the children of Israel, or the children of Jacob.

Jacob had twelve children and was so loved by God that he changed his name to Israel, which literally means 'he who struggled with God', which may be interpreted as 'God's hero'. During this time, there was an awful famine in Canaan, so Jacob and his twelve children went to Egypt and settled in Goshen, on the Nile River. The Hebrews flourished in Egypt and the bible tells us that one of Jacob's sons, Joseph, became deputy to Pharaoh, the Egyptian king, who told Joseph: *"thou shalt be over my house, and according to thy word shall all my people be ruled, only in the throne will I be greater than thou"*.

The Jews remained in Egypt for about four hundred years, where they grew in number and became prosperous. The new Egyptian kings, who did not know Joseph, viewed their success with envy and decided to put them down; the Hebrews were now made slave workers to build new towns and other Egyptian projects. However, as often happens in dire times, a great leader by the name of Moses rose up from the oppressed and led his people to freedom. Moses took the Hebrews out of Egypt and led them to their Promised Land, Canaan. He could have brought them directly along the Mediterranean coastline, but it seemed that he preferred to roam about in the desert for forty years, until most of the slave generation have died out and a new free generation has taken over. It has been calculated that the Exodus, the departure of the Hebrews from Egypt, took place about 1290 B.C. Moses brought to his people the ten commandments and made laws, 'Torah', for almost every aspect of life, as how to worship God, what food to eat [kosher], what food is unhealthy and prohibited, the obligation to respect one's parents, the order to farmers not to glean their crops but to leave something for the poor, as well as many other humane precepts, such as *"thou shall not hate your brother in thine heart"*, *"thou shall not avenge nor bear any grudge"* and the finest of all laws: *"thou shalt love thy neighbour as yourself"*.

Moses died at the eastern bank of the Jordan River around 1250 B.C, before entering the Promised Land of Canaan. He left the command to Joshua, one of his talented officers, under whose leadership the Hebrews overran the land east of the Jordan, crossed the river, and captured the city of Jericho, which was fortified with a gigantic wall. Joshua was a great leader and a brilliant warrior. He went on conquering hill after hill and town after town until all the land of Canaan was in his hands, except the plains, which were in the hands of the philistines, a tribe from the island of Crete that invaded Canaan and settled on its coastline. Joshua divided the conquered land among the twelve tribes of Israel, which were the descendants of the twelve sons of Jacob and bore their names. i.e., Reuben, Simeon, Levi, Judah, Zebulun, Issachar, Dan, Gad, Asher, Naphtali, Joseph and Benjamin.

Between Joshua and the prophet Samuel, a period of about 200 years, the twelve tribes of Israel lived separately and did not have a king to rule over them as the other nations. During this period, temporary leaders, called Judges, "judged" [ruled over] the Israelites. The Judges were heroes who sprang out in calamitous times, when the Jewish tribes were threatened or oppressed by an enemy. They were exceptional warriors who fought and delivered their people from the oppression of hostile tribes that dwelled at the time in Canaan and its neighbourhood. Among the most known Judges were:

Barak, who defeated the army of the Canaanites with their nine hundred chariots of iron. The battle took place at the foot of Mount Tabor where all the Canaanite soldiers were slain and not a man left, except Sisera, the captain of their army, who fled away on foot to the tent of Jael. The exhausted Sisera was then slain by Jael after he fell asleep.

Gideon, who, with only 300 hundred men delivered his people from the oppression of the Midianites and slew their two kings, Zebah and Zalmuna. The men of Israel then asked Gideon to rule over them and Gideon replied: *"I will not rule over you, neither my son will rule over you, but the Lord shall rule over you"*.

Samson, the most famous of all Judges, was endowed with unusual strength. He defeated the Philistines in numerous skirmishes, but he was betrayed by his lover, Delilah, and imprisoned by the Philistines. During a mocking ceremony, Samson bent the pillars of the house with his unusual strength, causing it to collapse on all the people therein. So, the number of Philistines that he slew in his death was greater than the number he slew in his life.

Deborah, the only female Judge was certainly an exception. She judged Israel at the time of the Canaanite oppression. Deborah sent for Barak and instructed him to summon ten thousand men to fight the Canaanite army, but Barak, despite being a brilliant and experienced fighter, was hesitant to go to war against the powerful Canaanites. He said to Deborah: *"If you will go with me, I will go; but if you will not go with me, I will not go"*. And she answered *"I shall surely go with you"*.

The era of the Judges lasted about 200 years, during which time the Jews saw periods of peace and others of wars and repression. They finally realized that their division into separate tribes had been the main cause of their weakness and started thinking of unity under one king.

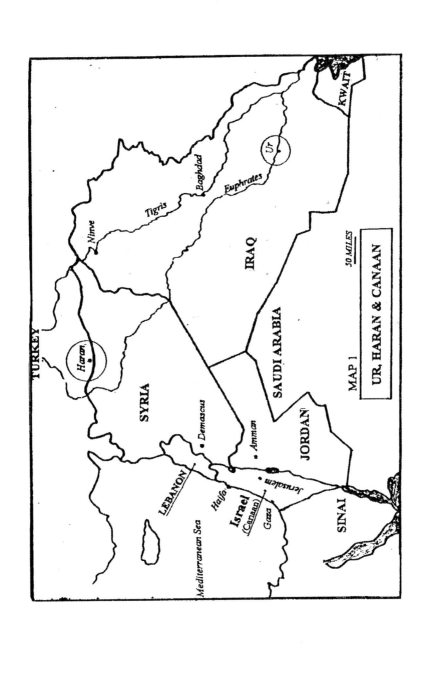

MAP 1

UR, HARAN & CANAAN

2

THE KINGDOM OF ISRAEL AND THE FIRST TEMPLE

Approximately in the year 1030 B.C. the Israelites wanted a king to rule over them *"like the other nations"*. Samuel, their religious leader and prophet, chose Saul, the son of a landowner named Kish, of the tribe of Benjamin, to be the first king of Israel. Saul proved to be a good warrior and his victories over the Philistines, Ammonites and Amalekites attested to his military capability. During that time, a brilliant young man called David captured the people's imagination when he smote Goliath, the giant Philistine foe, with a single stone shot with his sling. The defeat of Goliath put the Philistines to flight and resulted in a great victory for Israel. David's later successes in the battlefield against the Philistines aroused Saul's jealousy. He underwent bouts of depression and attempted to slay David with his own hands. Saul reigned for about 20 years and met his tragic end in a disastrous battle with the Philistines on Mount Gilboa, where his beloved son Jonathan also perished.

David succeeded Saul as king of Israel in about 1010 B.C when he was 30 years old and ruled for 40 years. He was a shepherd from the tribe of Judah, the eighth and youngest son of Jesse of Bethlehem. David was handsome and had red hair. He served King Saul from time to time as a harp player and armour bearer. His heroic battles against the philistines made David the favourite of the people, to Saul's envy and anger. For several years David was on the run and moved to the hill country of Judah in order to escape the wrath of Saul. After the Latter's death, David was anointed king of Judah in Hebron, where upon a civil war broke out between the supporters of David and those of Saul's only surviving son, Ish-Bosheth. The war lasted seven years with the victory of David and the assassination of Ish-Bosheth, and David was finally anointed king over all Israel.

David captured the fortress of Zion from the Jebusites and moved his capital from Hebron to Jerusalem. He was certainly Israel's greatest king and during his reign he made great territorial gains that stretched his kingdom from the Nile River in Egypt to the Euphrates River. But power corrupted him. He coveted a beautiful married woman, Bathsheba, and sent her husband, Uriah, to the front to be killed on the battlefield. The Prophet Nathan admonished King David in a clever way. He asked the King what should be done to a rich man who had stolen his poor neighbour's lamb for a banquet to his guest. The king said: *"The man that has done this should surely die"* and Nathan replied: *"Thou art that Man"*.

Later, when David was much older, a civil war broke out when his son, Absalom, attempted to usurp the kingdom from his father. Despite his human faults and foibles, David was, and remained, the most admired and beloved king of Israel. He died at the age of seventy after having reigned for forty years and was buried in Jerusalem, known as the City of David.

David chose Solomon, his tenth son, to succeed him to the crown. Solomon's coronation, which was urged by the prophet Nathan and his mother Bathsheba, took place before his father's death. He became well known because of his wisdom, his brilliant judgments, and because of the magnificent Temple of God, which he built in Jerusalem, and in which he placed the Ark of the Covenant, containing the Ten Commandments. Solomon also carried out numerous other projects in his kingdom, whose magnificence and splendour was unrivalled anywhere. He built ships and traded with Spain, India and the coasts of Africa. During his 40 years reign, Israel's twelve tribes were united as one nation in a powerful and prosperous kingdom, with Jerusalem as its Capital.

After Solomon's death, the kingdom of Israel split in two. The Northern kingdom maintained the name 'Israel'. It included ten of the twelve tribes and established its capital in Samaria. The Southern kingdom was called 'Judah'; it consisted of the remaining two tribes, Judah and Benjamin, and had Jerusalem as its capital. Consequently, the Jews from the northern kingdom were called Israelites and those from the southern kingdom, Judeans, or Jews. The two kingdoms were never again as powerful as that of David or Solomon. Other powerful kingdoms, like Egypt and Assyria (northern today's Iraq) dominated the region. Prophets like Isaiah and Jeremiah saw the dangers coming and realised that neither Israel nor Judah could withstand an invasion from these powers. They preached for careful diplomacy and warned against any alignment, but in 721 B.C the Assyrians, under the command of their king, Saragon II, invaded Israel and over-ran it. They captured its capital, Samaria, razed down the Jewish northern kingdom, killed its population and deported those who survived. The kingdom of Israel existed for about 210 years, from the split of Solomon's kingdom in about 930 B.C. until its destruction by the Assyrians. The annihilation was so complete that it disappeared completely from the surface of the earth.

Meanwhile a rising new power called Babylonia (southern today's Iraq) destroyed the mighty Assyria. Their king, Nebuchadnezzar II, marched with his troop on Judah in the year 586 B.C, conquered it, destroyed Jerusalem, ransacked Solomon's magnificent Temple and burned it to the ground. Nearly all the Jews were deported, except for a few people who remained among the ruins of Jerusalem. During the 440 years of its existence, the kingdom of Judah has known greatness and magnificence as well as decline and degradation. It had been ruled by a dynasty of talented and brilliant kings as well as mediocre and rash ones, it had periods of peace and periods of wars, abundance and shortage, and finally, 700 years after the Exodus from Egypt, once again the Jews found themselves exiles, this time on the banks of the Euphrates and Tigris Rivers.

3

THE DESTRUCTION OF THE SECOND TEMPLE

The Exiles in Babylonia continued to mourn for their homeland, their kingdom, Jerusalem, the Temple and the holy sites. They used to meet on Sabbath and read from the book of the Torah, Moses' Law, which they brought along with them. These meetings, or gatherings, were called 'Knesset' in Hebrew, or 'synagogue' in Greek, and thus were the beginning of prayers and synagogue buildings that followed thereafter. The Babylonian exile lasted fifty years.

One great power declines and another arises. This time it was the Persians who stormed from the east and conquered Babylonia. In 538 B.C., the Persian king, Cyrus, allowed several thousands of Jews to return to their homeland and rebuild their Temple in Jerusalem. The returning exiles worked on the temple over 20 years and finally completed it in 515 B.C. During the years that followed, two great Jewish leaders, Nehemiah and Ezra, arrived from Persia. Nehemiah arrived in Jerusalem in about 445 B.C, but Ezra's arrival time is uncertain, and is believed to have taken place some years after Nehemiah. Both leaders were pious and dedicated to the Law of Moses, yet they differed in their contribution to their people, for Nehemiah was an administrator, while Ezra was a devout priest. Nehemiah was appointed by King Cyrus as governor of the 'province of Judah', responsible for law and order and for the rebuilding of Jerusalem. Ezra, on the other hand, did everything possible to strengthen the religion. He taught and explained the Torah in Aramaic, the spoken language at the time, and appointed scribes to teach the law and make manuscript copies of the bible, so that it would be available to all the people.

In a world of paganism and idolatry, the Jews held to their belief in one God and recited this belief in their daily prayers: *"Hear Oh Israel, the Lord our God, the Lord is one".* There is little doubt that thanks to the work of these two outstanding leaders, the number of the returning exiles grew and they became strong, organised, hard working, self supportive, trained to defend themselves, repulsed by the surrounding customs of idolatry and dedicated to their own religion and law. With the contribution of Ezra and Nehemiah the Jews remained united in their faith and religion for many centuries thereafter. This strong bond helped them to survive two thousand years of non-statehood, while bigger and mightier nations disappeared without trace.

Meanwhile, another legendary military star arose in the skies of the region. Alexander the Great captured the mighty kingdoms of Egypt and Persia in 331 B.C. together with all their provinces, including Judah. After his death in 323 B.C., two of his generals ruled the region. Ptolemy took over Egypt and Seleucids ruled in Asia. For over one hundred years the Judeans were subjects of the Ptolemys, who were tolerant and allowed the Jews to practise their own faith and elect their own high priest. But in 198 B.C. the Greek king Antiochus of Syria captured Judea and gradually started enforcing the Greek way of life. He ordered the Jews to reject their God and to worship Zeus. He outlawed the Torah and circumcision, desecrated the Temple and erected a statue of Zeus on the altar.

In 168 B.C. The Jews revolted under the leadership of a priest called Mattetyahu [Mattathias] the Hasmonaite, of the Hasmonaean family, and his five sons, Judah, John, Simeon, Eleazar and Jonathan. Judah was the hero of the revolt and his strikes against the Greeks earned him the title of 'Maccabee', which means 'The Hammerer'. The fighting lasted for about four years and ended up in the defeat of the Greek Syrians and their expulsion from Judea. The Maccabeans cleansed the Temple from the pagan symbols, lit the lamps of the Great Menorah, and resumed their worship of God in the holy Temple in Jerusalem. The Maccabean brothers became a dynasty that ruled over Judea for many years. Under their relatively long reign they have enlarged the boundaries of the country and the Jews lived independently, at least from the religious aspect, for many years to come.

A nice legend followed the victory of the Maccabeans: when they entered the Temple, they found only a small jug of oil that would keep the lamp lit for not more than one day, but a miracle occurred and the lamp stayed lit for eight days. Since then, the Jews celebrate 'Hanukkah', which means 'inauguration', to mark the victory of the Maccabees and the re-inauguration of the Temple. The festival lasts eight days to commemorate the oil miracle.

The decline of the Greeks saw the rise of the Romans and brought Syria under their domination. In 63 B.C., the Roman General Pompey captured Jerusalem and recognised Hyrcanus, the great grandson of Simeon the Maccabean, as ethnarch (leader in Greek) of the Jews, but he reduced his authority by appointing Antipater, an Edumean who was Jewish by religion though not by birth, as the Procurator. His son, Herod, was popular with the Romans and was eventually made king of Judah, now known as Judea. Herod was a good king; he carried out large building and architectural projects in Jerusalem, Jericho and Caesarea, such as fortifications, theatres, arenas, and most importantly the rebuilding of the Temple, which was destroyed and plundered by Pompey's soldiers.

During his 40 years of reign there was peace and prosperity. The Jewish population in Judea flourished to about 2.5 millions, in addition to about 1 million in Babylonia and 4.5 millions scattered in other provinces of the Roman Empire.[1] Jewish scholars, such as Hilel and Shammai, taught the Bible and contributed a great deal to its interpretation, and Jewish religious life around the holy Temple of God was at its peak. On the other hand, Herod was a suspicious and violent king. He ordered the execution of many of his citizens, including his Maccabean wife, Miriam, and two of his sons, with no reason other than rashness and rage. Despite the fact that he was a practising Jew, and in spite of his desperate attempts to win over the people's favour and support, the Jews considered him Edumean and a foreigner and hated him in his life as well as on his death, which took place in 4 B.C. It is worth remembering that Herod the Great had nothing to do with Jesus, for he died 4 years before Jesus was born. The verse in Matthew 2:13-15 that *"Herod is determined to hunt the child down and destroy him"* probably refers to Herod's son, Herod Antipas, who, after his father's death became the Ruler of Galilee and the East Bank of the Jordan. Jesus despised Herod Antipas and compared him to a fox, an animal that was considered cunning and unclean.

In 66 AD another revolt, much greater than that of the Maccabeans, broke out in Judea. This time against the Romans. The cause of the revolt was the Roman Procurator, Gessius Florus, who, out of personal greed, robbed the Temple of its treasures. When the Jews protested, Florus ordered his soldiers to kill many innocent people. In response to this atrocity, the Jews retaliated by seizing the Temple and wiping out the Roman garrison in Jerusalem. The rebellion spread like fire in a cotton field, to the North and to the South of Judea, from Galilee to the Dead Sea. Jewish Commanders were appointed in each province. Joseph Ben-Mattetiahu, who later changed his name to Flavius Joshephus and became a famous historian, was appointed commander of Galilee. The rebels recruited fighters from all districts of Judea and took control of strongholds and fortified towns. Florus asked Rome for help. An army was sent from Syria to Jerusalem, but it was beaten and driven back. Following this defeat, the Roman emperor, Neron, sent an army of about 60,000 well-trained soldiers to Galilee, under the command of General Vespasian and his son Titus.

The Romans advanced in Galilee meeting fierce resistance. After a brave and desperate fight, the Jews of Galilee had no other choice but to surrender to a much superior, and well-armed force. With the advance of the Romans, Joseph Ben-Mattetiahu retreated to the fortified town of Yodpat [Jotapata]. He fought there with great valour even when his fortress had been besieged by the Romans and ran out of food and supplies. Eventually, the Romans broke through the walls of the town and killed almost all the starved defenders. Ben-Mattetiahu hid in a cave and when he was found he prophesised that General Vespasian would soon become Emperor. When his prophecy came true, Joseph Ben-Mattetiahu was brought to the Roman

Palace in great honour, where upon he changed his name to Flavius Josephus (Flavius being the first name of Vespasian) and became a famous historian under the patronage of the Emperor, who took power in 69 AD, the year known as the year of the four emperors, i.e., Nero, Galba, Vetilius and Vespasian, all four succeeding each other in just one year.

But the rebellion did not end with the fall of Galilee, for the survivors fled southwards to Jerusalem. Titus took over command from his father, who had been called to Rome to become Emperor. He advanced his forces to Jerusalem and laid siege to it. His plan was to starve the population behind the walls of the beleaguered city. After five months of siege, the Romans breached the city's wall, but the Jews continued to fight with great courage. The Romans advanced step by step, pushing the zealots back into the city and setting the Temple on fire. The zealots did not give up and continued to fight, but gradually the Romans occupied the entire city and Jerusalem fell into their hands. The Temple was destroyed except for its Western wall that became a shrine to the Jewish people and a 'Wailing Wall' at which they mourned the destruction of their kingdom and Temple for many centuries to come, until this very day. The plundered treasures of the Temple, together with many of the Jewish captives, were dragged along in a victory parade in Rome. The Romans commemorated Titus' victory by erecting the Arch of Titus in the centre of their capital. Some of the treasures and the captives can still be seen carved on a relief on the walls of the Arch.

The Romans continued their attacks and destroyed many other fortresses south and east of Jerusalem, but the rebels did not give up yet. Eleazar Ben Ya'eer, a zealot and staunch enemy of the Romans, still held the important and strong fortress of

Masada, together with about 1,000 men, women and children. The fortress was almost impregnable. Herod the Great built it as a resort palace on a steep cliff in the Judean desert, overlooking the Dead Sea. After a two-year siege, a ramp was built on the western wall of the fortress, and by April 73 AD the Romans were ready to attack. Realizing the approaching end, Ben Ya'eer summoned his people, explained to them the dire situation, and suggested that they should take their lives with their own hands rather than fall in the hands of the Romans and be sold as slaves in Rome.[2,3] Consequently, when the Romans entered the fortress, they found the dead bodies of the defenders; 960 men, women and children who preferred to die rather than become slaves. Only two women and five children survived to tell the story; they *"had hidden in the conduits that brought drinking-water underground, while the rest were intent upon the suicide-pact"*.[2] In the early nineteen-sixties, the late professor Yigael Yadin excavated the fortress and found skeletons of the defenders. He also found traces of Herod's palace, a synagogue, coins minted during the revolt, personal possessions, food jars, as well as many other artefacts pertaining to the great revolt of a small nation against a powerful empire.[3] With the fall of Masada, the seven years' revolt came to an end. Many thousands of Jews died in the fighting, many others were sold as slaves and only some remained on the scorched land to hold the Jewish flame in their homeland.

4

JUDEA RENAMED 'PHILISTIA'

After the Great Revolt of 66-73 AD, the number of Jews who had remained in Judea had increased and they were joined by many others who returned to their destroyed homeland. They lived in relative peace under the Roman occupation. The Roman Emperor, Trajan, promised the Jews that he would rebuild Jerusalem and their temple and in return the Jews undertook not to revolt and to maintain quiet in Judea. When Hadrian succeeded Trajan in 117 AD, he was a benevolent despot and treated the Jews with sympathy and respect. His nephew, Aquilas, even converted to Judaism. Hadrian visited Jerusalem in order to see the site that his predecessor promised to rebuild for the Jews, and was appalled by the ruin and desolation of the once flourishing city. He immediately expressed his intention to rebuild Jerusalem and the Temple. However, it soon transpired that Hadrian's intention was to rebuild Jerusalem as a Hellenistic city and to place an altar for the pagan god, Jupiter, in the Temple that he was going to rebuild, and appoint himself as the high priest. Hadrian added insult to injury by prohibiting circumcision. The Jews felt disgraced, insulted and mocked and saw in these actions an intention to Romanise Judea.

That was the last straw that broke the camel's back and triggered a revolt in 132 AD. Simon Bar-Kochba was the Jewish leader of this insurrection, encouraged and supported by the spiritual leader rabbi Akiva. Bar-Kochba recruited a large army, mainly among the Jews of Judea, though a number of recruits arrived from other Jewish centres as well. He defeated the Romans, captured Jerusalem and some other fifty towns and many villages. Bar Kochba declared the independence of Judea from Rome, placed the altar where it used to stand in the Temple, minted Judean coins and started building a wall around Jerusalem. Having been so humiliated, Hadrian sent a large force under the command of his most competent general, Julius Severus, whom he drew out of a campaign in England[4]. Severus recaptured fortress after fortress and town after town, first in Galilee and then around Jerusalem, pushing the rebels back into their last fortified town of Bethar, not far from Jerusalem. Bar Kochba was killed during the fighting over Bethar, and the rest of the defenders, having been starved and demoralised, surrendered to the superior Roman army.

The results of the revolt were disastrous to the Jews.[43] It is believed that over half a million had been killed during the insurrection, the siege and the fall of Bethar in August 135 AD.[1] The survivors were sold as slaves, others left Judea and settled elsewhere, and many fled to Galilee, where they established a large centre of the surviving Jews. Hadrian expunged the names of Judea and Jerusalem from the map of the Roman Empire. He rebuilt Jerusalem but recalled it Aelia Capitolina after his own first name (Aelius). He also changed the name of the Jewish homeland, Judea, to 'Philistia' (which later became Palestine), after the Philistine tribe from Crete that battled with the Jewish Kings many centuries before Hadrian and had since disappeared from the surface of the earth. The Jewish independent homeland had now been destroyed and was not to rise again until 18 centuries later. During the excavations by professor Yigael Yadin In 1960, 15 papyrus letters by Bar Kochba were found in a cave near the Dead Sea. They were written in a concise and hasty manner and were mostly orders by the chief commander, Bar Kockba, to some of his officers.[4, 5]

5

THE DIASPORA

Although the independence of Judea came to an end with the fall of Bethar in 135 AD and most of the Jews were driven out or fled to other countries in Europe and Asia, there always remained a religious diehard core in Palestine, practising their religion and praying for the reconstruction of their Temple. One of the large Jewish communities lived in Babylonia, and a smaller one in Palestine, both producing famous scholars in the study of the Bible and its teaching. In the third century a large volume of commentary on the law books of the Bible was concluded. It contained exegeses of laws and rules that were passed orally from father to son through the centuries and were now sorted out and collated in a volume, called 'Mishna', which means 'reciting' or 'learning'. With the passage of years, the rabbis found that the 'Mishna' itself had to be explained. Through hard and lengthy work, simultaneously in Babylonia and Palestine, two versions of interpretation of the 'Mishna' were produced at the end of the 5th century. These volumes were called 'Talmud', which means 'teaching'. The one produced in Babylonia (the Babylonian Talmud) is considered more comprehensive and therefore is more widely studied by Jewish law students and Rabbis.

The Jews who fled to Europe knew periods of calm and others of persecution alternately. Those who were lucky to live in any of the large areas under the reign of Charlemagne (the great Frank ruler who died in 814 AD and reigned over most of Western Europe of today) were respected and well treated. They mostly dealt with trade and commerce and became prosperous, to the extent that the regular market in the city of Lyon was changed from Saturday to a weekday, as the Jews would not work on Sabbath.[1] But, when Europe started to disintegrate into small provinces governed by kings, princes or petty despots, the Jews were reliant on the caprice of these rulers and were often deprived of their rights, excluded from certain trades or studies, and sometimes even expelled. In quiet times, however, the Jews thrived, opened their own academies for the study of the Bible and the Talmud and produced great scholars. The famous Jewish traveller, Benjamin of Tudela (a city in northern Spain), spent 13 years, from 1160 to 1173 AD, travelling from one Jewish community to another in Europe and North Africa, recording their conditions in his diary, which became a reliable historical source of Jewish life during that era.

The period of the Crusades brought hard times to the Jews. In the year 1095 fanatic Muslims in Palestine attacked and killed Christian pilgrims, desecrated Jesus' tomb and ransacked the church of the Holy Sepulchre, leaving it in ruins. Pope Urban II spoke in the city of Clermon (central France) and called for a crusade to free Jerusalem and save the church of the Holy Sepulchre from the hands of the infidels. The response was immense. Even Pope Urban had not dreamt that his call would mobilise such great numbers to the crusade. However, not all of the volunteers had Jesus in their minds and a large number of peasants and serfs who joined the march eastwards did it for adventure and plunder. Such men bundled their families on carts, with a few personal possessions, and started streaming eastwards without even knowing where exactly Palestine was. On their way, they were stirring up hatred against the Jews, saying *"why wait until we reach Palestine [to punish the Muslim infidels], we can punish the infidels [Jews] here and now. Let's kill God's enemies"*. A series of massacres took place in France and Germany and only a few Jews were given the choice to leave their property and be baptised or face death. When they refused, they were murdered in cold blood.

Whole Jewish communities were wiped out altogether. The law was in the hands of the rabble. And finally, the Crusaders reached Jerusalem in 1099 and laid siege to it.[6,31] The Jews of Jerusalem fought together with the Muslims in the defence of the city, but when it fell in the hands of the Crusaders, all of them were massacred, Muslims and Jews alike.[6]

The second Crusade passed with relatively few killings, but the third Crusade (1191-1192 AD) of King Richard the first of England, known as the Lion Heart, was soaked in Jewish blood. The mob was enflamed with false accusations and blood libels, such as the use of Christian children's blood by the Jews to make their unleavened bread during Passover. King Richard tried to stop this incitement, but as soon as he left on his crusade to Palestine the mob started attacking Jewish life and property. In the city of York, about five hundred Jews barricaded themselves in a castle, fighting back bravely and choosing to kill themselves rather than surrender to the crusaders. The killing extended to other parts of the city and almost the whole Jewish population of York was wiped out. The sad saga of the Jews of England came to an end about a century later, when in 1290 King Edward I expelled all of them, and they were not to return until the time of Cromwell in the 17th century.

The lesson learned by the Jews from the Crusades was that property can easily be ransacked or destroyed, but money is easier to save. Consequently, the Jews became moneylenders. However, in England and Europe, the rulers determined the interest on the lent money, and since a large portion of the interest ended up in their pockets, they often fixed high rates. If the rulers needed more money, they scrounged it from the collectors (the Jews) and when these became destitute, it was time to expel them. It reached such absurdity that, sometimes, after the Jews were expelled they were allowed to return, providing they paid for the right to return. But when they paid and returned, they found that their houses were confiscated and their possessions looted.[1]

For centuries to come, the Jews of Europe suffered attacks on their property, pogroms, massacres and expulsions. The Christians always found a false accusation to instigate violence against the Jews. It was often the favourite blood libel, a ritual murder, or in certain occasions, as during the Black Death (1348-1349), the Jews were accused of infecting the water well, causing a disastrous epidemic. The fact that the disease smote Christians and Jews alike had no effect upon Christians' logic, their hatred of the Jews and desire for plunder were much stronger.

The only exception in Europe was Spain under the Muslim rule (710-1492 AD), where the Jews were generally well treated. The Moors, as the Spanish Muslims were called, allowed the Jews to practise their religion freely, and enter any type of profession they chose. This period in Jewish history is known as the 'Golden Age' and had lasted for about 400 years, until in

1145 AD Spain was captured by a fanatic Muslim Berber sect
from Morocco, called al-Mohades [distorted from the Arabic
name 'al-Muwahidun', meaning the 'Unitarians'], who offered
the Christians and the Jews a choice between Conversion to
Islam, death or exile. During the Golden Age, however, several
Jewish academies were founded in Cordova, Granada and other
cities in Spain, producing a long chain of famous Jewish
scholars, philosophers, doctors, writers, poets and diplomats. It
would be remiss not to mention just a few of them, such as
Hasdai ibn Shaprut, born 915 AD, who became the Caliph's
personal doctor, advisor and personal envoy on diplomatic
missions; Samuel ibn Nagrela, born 993 AD, a writer and a
poet, so much admired by the Caliph that he was brought to the
court, granted a title of 'Nagid' [Prince] and appointed Chief
Minister, a post second only to the Caliph; Solomon ibn
Gabirol, born 1021, a poet, astronomer and philosopher;
Jehuda Halevi, born 1095, a doctor and the greatest Jewish poet
of his time, whose poems were a powerful expression of the
Jewish yearning to return to their historic homeland; Moses
Maimonedes, born 1035 in Cordova, a brilliant writer,
philosopher and famous doctor, who became the personal
physician of Saladin, Egypt's great ruler and hero of Islam.

In Christian Spain, the persecution of the Jews was mainly
religious and their lives could sometimes be spared if they
converted. Many Jews opted to convert but observed their
Judaism in secret. The Church was dissatisfied with the loyalty
of the converts and believed that a more drastic measure should
be taken against them. Consequently, Queen Isabella and King
Ferdinand established the Inquisition in order to uncover the
false converts, or 'Conversos' as they were called, who were
suspected of disloyalty to Christianity, and punish them

severely. Perhaps the most famous 'Conversos' were the rich and influential Mendes family, who owned several banks in Spain and other countries in Europe. The heiress of that wealth was a beautiful widow by the name of Gracia [known as Dona Gracia], who fled from Spain together with her daughter, Reina, and her Nephew, Joseph Nasi, to Antwerp, where she became close to the Royal Court. Eventually she was again suspected of disloyalty to Christianity and had to flee, this time to Venice, where she was arrested on a charge of abandoning her Christian faith. Dona Gracia's nephew, Joseph, a brilliant young man, had secretly passed an urgent message to the powerful Sultan of the Ottoman Empire, whose name alone instilled fear in Europe. When the Sultan announced that Dona Gracia was under his protection, the Venetians hastened to free her and give her back all her money and property. The three members of the Mendes family then arrived in Istanbul and reconverted to Judaism. Gracia dedicated the rest of her life to the benefit of her people, and Reina married her cousin, Joseph, who eventually became the Foreign Minister of the Turkish Empire.

Under the Inquisition, many Jews were put to death, and those who were not burnt at the stake, suffered awful punishment and tortures. The Inquisition was, nevertheless, dissatisfied and wanted the total banishment of the Jews from Spain. Consequently, in 1492, the same year that Christopher Columbus discovered America, the king and queen of Spain yielded to the Inquisition's pressure and issued a decree for the expulsion of the Jews from Spain within four months. Those who stayed beyond this period risked the death penalty.

Most of the Jewish fugitives left for Italy and Portugal, from where they were expelled again at a later stage. Some Jews left for North Africa and from there to Palestine, where they established a Jewish settlement in Safed (Upper Galilee), which eventually became a famous centre of the Talmud and Kabala. A large number of the Spanish Jews arrived in Turkey and were received with open arms by the Muslim Sultan, for there were among them many financiers, scholars, craftsmen and artisans, who contributed a great deal to the economy and welfare of the Muslim Sultanate. As to Spain, no Jews were allowed to live there until 1808, when Napoleon Bonaparte abolished the Inquisition.

In the year 1492, the same year that the Jews were expelled from Spain, the Arab Moors faced a similar fate when they lost their last bastion of Granada to the Spanish Christian forces. Like the Jews, the Arabs had been in Spain for many centuries, but contrary to the Jews who had been loyal and helpful citizens, the Arabs arrived in Spain as conquerors in the 8th Century and since had been warring with the native Christians, who sought to expel them. The conquest of Granada and the expulsion of the Moors by the Christians marked, therefore, the victorious conclusion of a long military conflict.

In Eastern Europe the Jews suffered the same dire fate. Poland, Ukraine and Russia were the most notorious for their treatment of Jews. Attacks on their property and pogroms forced the Jews to move from one country to another in search of security. In 1656 Cromwell allowed the re-admittance of Jews into England despite the objection of his Council of State. Although they were not granted full rights, they were well treated, allowed to trade freely, to open Jewish schools and synagogues and practice their religion without restrictions. With time, the Jews of England prospered and produced distinguished leaders, such as Disraeli (a Jew by birth, converted after his Bar Mitsvah) who became twice Prime Minister and was Queen Victoria's favourite; Sir Moses Montefiore who was knighted by Queen Victoria; and Lionel de Rothschild, whose son Nathaniel became a peer and the first Jew to sit in the House of Lords in 1885.

America was also a safe haven for Jewish fugitives. They arrived in small numbers during the 17th century and settled in New York, Rhode Island, Newport, the colonies of Pennsylvania, North and South Carolina and Georgia. After the American War of Independence, the Jews were granted full citizenship and became equal before the Law. Towards the end of the nineteenth century, vast numbers of Jewish immigrants entered into the United States. Most of these penniless and destitute immigrants were fleeing persecution in Russia, coming out of their poor and crowded ghettos and landing in the vastness and opulence of the New World. Leaving behind oppression and humiliation to find freedom and dignity. They were indeed the *"tired, poor, huddled masses yearning to breathe free"* whom the American-Jewish poet, Emma Lazarus, described in her celebrated poem 'The New Colossus'. Upon arrival of the immigrants, Jewish friends, relatives and charities supported and helped them in finding accommodation and work in various trades and factories. The employers often exploited the new immigrants, who had to work long hours for ridiculously low wages. But, through hard work and perseverance they achieved better conditions and wages. The second and third generations of these immigrants were sent to universities, acquired high education and adopted the American way of life, reaching, in many cases, high positions in the American administration.

On the other hand, the Jews of Europe had to wait for Napoleon Bonaparte to obtain their emancipation. In 1804 Napoleon crowned himself Emperor of France and made one of his most important contributions, the Civil Code, which applied the maxim of the French Revolution "Liberty, Equality and Fraternity" to all subjects, including the Jews.[7] This decision was remarkable in view of the prejudice and discrimination that were rampant at the time, and its importance was magnified in respect of the Jews, because it was adopted by many European countries that were under the occupation of Napoleon, after the downfall of the Holy Roman Empire.

Napoleon had never seen a Jew until he was 28 years old. This was in 1797, during his astounding victories over the Austrians in Italy. One day, when he was strolling in Ancona (Italian city on the Adriatic Sea), Napoleon noticed some people wearing yellow bands with the Star of David on their arms. His officers told him that they were Jews and the bands were for identification, so that they would not stay outside the Ghetto in the evening. The young general gave orders to remove the yellow bands, close the ghetto and allow the Jews to choose where to live, and grant them freedom to practice their religion. In a conversation with his private Irish physician, Dr. Barry O'Meara, on 10 January 1916, while in exile in St. Helena, Dr. O'Meara asked Napoleon about his sympathy to the Jews, and recorded Napoleon's answer in his memoir:

"My primary desire" said Napoleon, *"was to liberate the Jews and make them full citizens. I wanted to confer upon them all the legal rights of equality, liberty and fraternity, as was enjoyed by the Catholics and the Protestants. It is my wish that the Jews be treated*

like brothers, as if we were all part of Judaism. As an added benefit, I thought that this would bring to France many riches because the Jews are numerous and they would come in large numbers to our country, where they would enjoy more privileges than in any other nation. Without the events of 1814 [his defeat and exile to the Island of Elba], most of the Jews of Europe would have come to France, where equality, fraternity and liberty awaited them and where they can serve the country like everyone else".

Napoleon's statement in St. Helena appears genuine in light of the fact that before granting emancipation to the Jews, he received commitments from their leaders that their religion would not prevent them from obeying the country's law, pay taxes and serve in the army.

After Napoleon's defeat in Waterloo in 1814, his reforms were abolished, except in France and Holland. However, slowly and gradually, the Jews were granted equal rights in most of the European countries—in 1830 in Belgium, in 1867 in the Austria-Hungary empire, in 1871 in Germany after the consolidation of the German states by Bismarck, and in 1874 in Switzerland. Also Portugal and Spain revoked the edict of expulsion by 1868, but Russia remained harsh on its Jewish population, increased their taxation and banned them from certain occupations. In 1891 the city of Moscow expelled all its Jews and soon thereafter other cities, like St Petersburg and Kharkov, followed suit. The government blamed the ailments of the country on the Jews, accusing them of spreading the cholera disease, inciting the mob against them. Consequently, the Jews of Kishinev were massacred in a brutal pogrom in 1903, and those of Kiev were expelled in 1910. The Government continued its incitement, causing a wave of anti-

Jewish rioting and attacks on their property. The Jewish suffering was so great that by 1914, when the First World War broke out, over two million Jews, out of the six million of Russia, had already left the country and sought refuge in England and the United States. In 1906, three years after the Kishinev pogrom, the Family of Golda Meir, a future prime minister of Israel, fled the Russian persecution and arrived in America when she was 8 years old.

Since the destruction of the second Temple by Titus and the dispersal of the Jews in Babylonia, Asia and Europe, the Jews clung to their religion with great devotion and in many cases chose to die, rather than convert to Christianity, or abandon their faith. Despite the harassment, discrimination, attacks on their property, expulsions and pogroms, they always bore the memory of Jerusalem and the Temple in their hearts. Wherever they were, they built their synagogues facing Palestine, so that they could pray with their eyes fixed to Jerusalem. In their prayers, they remembered Jerusalem and longed for their return to their homeland as an independent free nation. In their weddings, the bridegrooms broke a glass with their foot in commemoration of the destruction of the Temple and recited the oath: *"If I forget thee Jerusalem, let my right arm forget her cunning"*. This unusual adherence to Judaism, religion and the scripture, as well as an ancient ancestors' decree that forbade the Jews to add or detract a word from the Bible, helped to maintain this small people through eighteen hundred difficult centuries of exile, while other nations, much bigger and mightier, had long disappeared from the surface of the earth.

6

MUHAMMAD AND ISLAM

Islam means 'submission', in this case to God. The Quran, the Muslim scripture, is believed by Muslims to be the miraculous utterance of God, delivered through revelations to his messenger Muhammad. The revelations, he alleged, were the true word of God, which he recited verbatim. The Quran consists of 114 Chapters, each called 'Sura', which means 'picture', for it depicts a revelation to the Prophet. The Suras are of different length and encompass not only religious, but also social, civil, commercial, military and legal codes. According to al-Khidri, professor of Islamic History at the Egyptian University of Cairo, Muhammad, the founder of Islam, was born on 8 June 570 AD in Mecca. His poor parents belonged to the Hashim clan, a branch of the most respectable and influential tribe of Quraysh. Muhammad's father, Abdullah, died a couple of months before he was born, and his mother, Amina, passed away when he was only six years old. His grandfather first took care of him, but after his death, his uncle, Abu Talib, took the boy into his house and brought him up as one of his children. Muhammad started his independent life as a camel driver, and through hard work and loyalty became a leader and a manager of a caravan.

Mecca, at the time, was an important prosperous oasis in the Arabian Desert, mainly because the Ka'aba, that enshrined the idols of the goddesses, was located there. Ka'aba means 'cubic' in Arabic, and the name describes the shape of the massive cubic, hollow, stone structure (50 ft. high, with a base of 35 by 40 ft.), in which a black meteoric stone, about 12 inches in diameter, is imbedded in one of its outside corners, 5 ft above the ground. The Ka'aba is today placed in the centre of Masjad al-Haram' [The Sacred Mosque], and together with its black stone, which was deemed sacred by Muhammad, is the holiest place of worship in Islam. It is also the centre of pilgrimage, which every Muslim is to do once in his life if possible, and is the 'Kibla' [direction] towards which Muslims all over the world face during their daily prayers.

At the time of Muhammad, the Meccans, as well as other tribes of Arabia, worshiped the goddesses that were placed in the Ka'aba. Mecca, therefore, attracted hordes of Pilgrims and the Meccans benefited financially from serving and selling goods to these Arab pilgrims during regular seasons and feasts. Secondly, Mecca was a junction between Egypt and Syria, providing services and trading with the caravans during their regular recreation stops at the oasis. Muhammad was known as an honest, trustworthy and able caravan manager. His good reputation made Khadija, a wealthy widow, entrust him to manage her business. Shortly afterwards, he accepted a proposal to marry her, when he was 25 years old and Khadija about 40.

Through his journeys with the caravan, and during commercial fairs in Mecca, Muhammad came in contact with Christians and Jews, and was thus introduced to the belief in one God and the tenets and faith of the 'People of the Book', as he later referred to them in the Quran. Being perplexed by what he had heard, Muhammad started to ponder about religious beliefs. He withdrew to a cave in Mount Hira, outside Mecca, to meditate and seek guidance. The Quran tells us that in one of his regular retreats, when he was 40 years old, the archangel Gabriel appeared in the cave and told him that he was chosen to be *"the messenger of God, the Creator of man and the Source of all knowledge, to proclaim his oneness universally"*. Muhammad's first followers were his wife and his cousin Ali, but as more revelations took place he started preaching among the people of Mecca. Facing rejection, resistance and later persecution, Muhammad fled Mecca to the city of Yathrib (later changed to 'Medina', which means 'City'), about 190 miles North of Mecca. The migration to Medina, known as the 'Hijra', took place in the year 622 AD, which had become the beginning of the Muslim Calendar.[8,9]

The Jews of Medina were about 60% of the total city's population at the time. When Muhammad arrived in the town, he tried to win the Jews onto his side and convince them that his mission was in line with their belief. He even faced Jerusalem when he prayed, like the Jews did all over the world. But, after they had rejected him, he started to face Mecca instead, a tradition which is practised by Muslims to this day. Later, however, the Jews paid dearly for their rejection, by expulsions, confiscation of their property and the mass killing of all the males of the Jewish tribe of Quraida (about 700 in number).[8,30,40] By the time the Prophet took complete control of Medina, the wealthy and prosperous Jewish tribes of that city had ceased to exist.

In Medina, Muhammad announced that God had now ordered him to fight the unbelievers. The Muslims' attacks were mainly on Meccan trade caravans. The battle of Bedr, the first skirmish between the Muslims and the Meccans, took place in 624 AD and was a decisive victory to the Muslims, in which 314 Muslims led by Muhammad defeated 1,000 Meccans. The second battle was fought at the foot of Mount Uhud in 625 AD, with 3,000 Meccans battling with 700 Muslims. Muhammad was wounded and the Muslims badly beaten and defeated, but the Meccans were not familiar with total war; instead of capturing Medina, as they easily could have done, they drove back to Mecca, threatening the Muslims with more retaliation if they misbehaved. In 630, Muhammad called the Meccans to arms. He set off to Mecca with 10,000 men, but the Meccans accepted Islam peacefully and without any resistance. Muhammad ordered the destruction of the idols. The Ka'aba, which was the centre of idolatry, became a holy shrine to the Muslims. The Prophet touched the black stone and performed the seven circuits around the Ka'aba as per the heathen ritual, which was since adopted by Islam.[8] In the year 632 AD, two years after the surrender of the Meccans and their conversion to Islam, the Prophet passed away and the reign passed to the Caliphs, the Islamic rulers who succeeded him.

Although the Muslims often refer to Muhammad as 'al-Nabi' [the prophet], he did not profess to be one. He alleged that he was a messenger, who was told to deliver the word of God, which he had received through revelations that were first committed to memory and later put down in written form in the Quran, in 650 AD. The Muslims believe that Muhammad was the last prophet and no other prophet will ever succeed him until doomsday.

The five pillars of Islam are the foundation of Muslim faith and life and only those who practise them are considered true Muslims; they are: Testimony (Shahada), Prayer (Salat), Charity (Zakah), Fasting (Sawm) and Pilgrimage (Hajj).

Testimony: A Muslim is one who testifies "there is no God but Allah and Muhammad is the messenger of Allah". By reciting this Testimony, anyone can become a Muslim, but if one later reneges, one could be considered an apostate.

Prayer: A Muslim is under the obligation to pray 5 times a day.

Charity: A Muslim calculates his own charity, but normally it is about 2.5% of his income.

Fasting: A Muslim should fast every day of the month of Ramadan, from dawn to sunset.

Pilgrimage: A physically and financially able Muslim is under the obligation to do the pilgrimage to Mecca, at least once in a lifetime.

Mecca is the holy city of Islam and the site of pilgrimage. Contrary to the Bible, in which Jerusalem was mentioned many hundreds of times, the Quran does not mention Jerusalem even once. The religious connection of the Muslims to Jerusalem does not clearly stem from the Quran, but rather from the Hadith, which is a collection of sayings attributed to the Prophet Muhammad. Sura 17 of the Quran, 'al-Isra' [which means 'to make someone go'], tells us about a night journey in which the Prophet was taken to 'Masjad al-Aqsa' [the remote temple] and brought back. The literal meaning of the Arabic word 'Masjad' is a place of worship, or a mosque. Sura 17 reads: *"Glory be to him who made his servant go by night from the sacred Masjad to the remote Masjad, whose surroundings We have blessed, that We might show him some of our signs..".*[26] The Quran does not say where that remote 'Masjad' was, but the Muslim interpretation of the 'sacred Masjad' is the 'Temple of Mecca', and that of the 'remote Masjad' is the 'Temple of Jerusalem'. However, the latter had been destroyed by Titus over five centuries before the time of Muhammad, and the al-Aqsa mosque would not be built until about a century thereafter.

As already said, the connection of Islam to Jerusalem comes mainly from the Hadith. Hadith means 'new' in Arabic, but this word also denotes 'news', 'a chat', 'a tale', 'a fable', 'a story', 'a legend', 'a report', etc. The Hadith is a collection of 'Sunnan', i.e., sayings, deeds or practices attributed to Muhammad, passed down from generation to generation by word of mouth, or in written form. It is a kind of supplement that elaborates on, and explains, the various revelations of the Quran. To Muslims, the Hadith is second in authority only to the Quran. It denotes the behaviour of the Prophet and sets a paradigm for Muslims to imitate. After the death of Muhammad, the number of hadiths transmitted through the generations reached astronomical figures, most of which were unreliable, fraudulent or spurious. Why would anyone want to fabricate a saying attributed to the Prophet? There were many reasons—for example: to promote or advocate an idea; to support or strengthen an opinion; to avoid punishment; to make a certain malicious gain; out of misguided motives, or from excessive zeal to glorify the Prophet, etc.[49,50]

It was reported that the famous scholar and collector, al-Bukhari, had collected some 600,000 hadiths by travelling and interviewing numerous people, but when he sorted them out he settled with only 2,600 original and genuine ones.[49,50] His collection 'al-Jami al-Sahih' [the correct collection] was compiled over 200 years after the death of Muhammad and is considered by most Muslims as the most important and reliable Hadith. In sorting out the true from the false, the Arab scholars found it necessary to examine each and every hadith on its own merits and reliability. It was probably the first scientific work of its kind ever carried out.

The scholars evaluated each 'hadith' by the honesty of the transmitter; his memory; his character and contacts; they also examined the place where he heard the hadith; from whom and when; whether it could be corroborated by others; whether it fitted in terms of place and time, etc. Out of hundreds of thousands, the scholars normally ended up with a few thousand reliable hadiths. These were compiled in the 2nd and 3rd centuries after the 'Hijra' (622 AD), when they were published. It is noteworthy to mention that there are quite a number of collections of Hadith and the Shia'as have their own collection. They generally do not recognize the Sunnis' collection and accept only those hadiths, which were passed down by the prophet's cousin, Ali, and his followers.

Various Hadith transmitters had narrated the 'Night Journey' in various versions. The essence of the story is that in the ninth year of the Prophet's mission, about 620 AD, the Prophet rose in the middle of the night to visit the Sacred Temple in Mecca. After a time of worship he fell asleep near the Ka'aba. The angel Gabriel came to him and woke him up from his slumber. He led the prophet to the edge of the sacred Meccan mosque. Awaiting them was al-Buraq, a white winged beast, *"bigger than a donkey but smaller than a mule"*, whose stride stretched from one horizon to another. Muhammad mounted al-Buraq and sped northwards with the angel Gabriel to the Remote Temple in 'Baytu al-Makdas', which in Arabic means 'the House of holiness', and interpreted as Jerusalem.

When they reached Jerusalem the Prophet dismounted and prayed in the mosque [there could not have been a mosque in Jerusalem at that time]. Abraham, Moses, Jesus and other prophets gathered to pray behind him. Muhammad was presented a vessel of wine and a vessel of milk. The Prophet chose the milk and Gabriel said: "you have chosen the true religion". The Prophet then embarked on the 'Miraj' [ascension], in which he received the command to pray five times a day.

Some European scholars expressed doubts about the genuineness of the Hadith and some believed that after Muhammad's death, his followers began to embellish the story of his life with mythology, and that the Prophet's ascension to heaven from Jerusalem was probably modelled on reports by the founders of other religions, such as the ascension of Jesus and the prophet Elijah to heaven. This opinion does not however make any difference to the devout Muslim who believes the Hadith to be a holy scripture and accepts it as second only to the Quran, just as a devout Christian would accept the gospel.

7

THE EXPANSION AND CONQUESTS OF ISLAM

After the death of Muhammad, the governing of the Muslim community was passed to the hands of able leaders called Caliphs, or 'Successors'. Contrary to the Prophet, who received revelations and delivered the Muslim Law (Sharia), the Caliphs had no power to promulgate dogma or change a tenet, for the revelation of the faith had been completed with the death of Muhammad. The issue of succession had, however, created a great dispute and caused a split between the main stream of the Sunna and the dissenters, which group was called 'Shia' (the Arabic word for 'Faction'). The Sunnis maintained that the Caliph should belong to the Quraish tribe, be elected by the representatives of the Muslim community, and be responsible for enforcing the religion and spreading Islam, by war if necessary. The Shiites agreed with the Sunnis about the duties of the Caliph, but maintained that not everyone can be chosen Caliph, for they believed the Prophet had selected Ali, his cousin and son-in-law, to succeed him, passing to him his divine spirit, sinlessness and infallibility. Consequently, only Ali's descendants, who are also Muhammad's descendants through his daughter Fatima, can succeed him as Caliphs and become supreme leaders of Islam.

This rift between the two main streams of Islam, the Sunnis and the Shia'as, exists to this very day. The Shia'as concept of Imamate is different from the Sunnis' concept of Caliph. To the Sunnis, the Caliph was the supreme leader, politically and militarily. The Shia'as, on the other hand, believe that the Imam is the supreme leader, in charge of religion and politics, and that he is divinely inspired. There are other significant differences between these two streams of Islam. For example, the Sunnis believe that God's revelations came to an end with the death of the Prophet Muhammad, while the Shia'as deem their leader to have the right to interpret the Quran and its enigmatic verses, because, they say that God would not leave his people without proper guidance. Also, the Shia'as believe in folk practices and saints; they consider intercession to be a necessary stage for salvation, for which Ali and the Imams can serve as intermediaries, while the Sunnis reject such practices and believe that the Muslims have direct relationship with God.

The Caliph's duty, as already mentioned, is to enforce the religion and spread Islam, by war if necessary. The obligation to fight in the way of Allah and Islam was mainly outlined in Sura 9, which is quoted below, and those who are slain in the cause of Allah and Islam *"He will vouchsafe them guidance and ennoble their estate; He will admit them to Paradise"* (Sura 47). Their heavenly rewards will include among others: immortal youths who shall wait on them *"with bowls and ewers and a cup of purest wine…with fruits of their own choice and flesh of fowls that they relish" (Sura 56); "bashful virgins as fair as corals and rubies, whom neither man nor Jinnie will have touched before" (Sura 55),* and *"dark-eyed houris, chaste as virgin pearls"*…whom God had created as *"loving companions for those on the right hand"* *(Sura 56).*

It is sometimes said that Islam is a peaceful religion. Some facts, however, do not seem to support this opinion. After the 'Hijra' [the immigration of Muhammad to Medina in 622 AD], for example, the Muslims under the leadership of Muhammad fought over 80 battles, with the Prophet taking part in all the major ones. Also, there are in the Quran some verses, and in the Hadith some passages attributed to Muhammad, that could not be considered peaceful, but are rather cruel and aggressive, especially against the Jews and Christians. Here are some examples that speak for themselves:

Sura 9—A verse in this Sura says: *"Fight those People of the Book [Jews and Christians] who do not believe in Allah and the last day, who do not prohibit what Allah and his apostle have forbidden, and do not embrace 'deen al-haq' [the true faith], until they pay the 'Jizya' [protective tax] and are utterly subdued".*

Sura 47—*When you meet the unbelievers in the battlefield strike off their heads..";*

Sura 5—It is said in this Sura that God had cursed the 'People of the Book' [the Jews and Christians] and transformed them into *"apes and swine";*

Sura 5— *"Those that deny our revelation We will burn in fire. No sooner will their skins be consumed than we shall give them fresh skins, so they must taste the torment";*

Sura 98—*"The unbelievers among the 'People of the Book' and the pagans shall burn for ever in the fire of hell. They are the vilest of all creatures",* i.e. the Jews and the Christians will specifically end up as the ember of hell. This reminds me that as a young boy in the Sudan, I was often shouted after by Muslims when passing by them: "O Jew! Ember of hell". At the time I knew it was a derogatory comment, but did not know that they were actually quoting from the Quran;

Sura 5—*"Believers, take neither Jews nor Christians for your friends…Whoever of you seeks their friendship shall become one of their number"*;

Hadith—*"The day of judgement will not come until the Muslims fight the Jews (killing the Jews), and when the Jews will hide behind stones or trees, the stones and trees will say: O Muslim, O Abdullah [Servant of Allah], there is a Jew behind me; come and kill him…."*. This passage, attributed to Muhammad (from the Hadiths of al-Bukhari and Muslim), constitutes part of the covenant of Hamas.

Hadith—The Prophet ordered to cut off the hands and legs of men belonging to the tribe of 'Ukl' and their eyes to be branded with heated pieces of iron, and their cut hands and legs (their bleeding limbs) not to be cauterised, till they died (Hadith by al-Bukhari, Volume 8, book 82, no.794).

Hadith—Uqba, who had been fighting with the Maccans in the battle of Bedr, was taken prisoner and condemned to death by the Prophet himself. Uqba begged for his life and cried: *"who will take care of my children?"* The Prophet replied: *"Hell fire"*[41]

Hadith—When certain poets of Medina wrote sarcastically about The Prophet, He caused three of them to be murdered by his disciples.[41]

These examples and especially the verse of Sura 9 quoted above, in which Muslims are called upon to fight the Jews and the Christians until they are utterly subdued, are certainly not conducive to peace. By contrast, the Old Testament, for example, commands us to treat people of other faiths equally and decently: *"If a stranger sojourns with thee in your land do not vex him. But a stranger that dwelleth with you shall be unto you as one born among you and thee shalt love him as thyself" (Leviticus, chapter 19:33,34)*

It is true to say that Muhammad, who had been humble and persecuted in Mecca, was transformed significantly after his arrival in Medina. He started using force in getting his way; he resorted to aggressive war against the Meccans; he expelled the Jewish tribe of Bani Qainuka into exile and confiscated their homes and property; he attacked Jewish towns, looted their riches and delivered them to Muslims; he approved the execution of all the 700 men of the Jewish tribe of Quraida, and arranged the murder of his opponents.

Verses of the Quran, like Sura 9 for example, served as a Jihad command to the Muslims and explained to them the aim of conquests. Other verses from the Quran and passages from the Hadith may have instigated the notorious Omar's Charter, or the Dhimma (writ of protection) aimed at protecting the Jews and the Christians against the Muslims themselves, in exchange for their subordination and tribute. People who were conquered by the Muslims were usually given the choice between death and conversion, but the Jews and Christians, known in the Quran as the 'People of the Book', were allowed to practise their faith with the explicit understanding that they were subjugated 'infidels', inferior to the Muslim believers. The Chart of Omar included a series of humiliating regulations, explicitly aimed to distinguish the Muslims as Masters and the Jews and Christians as slaves. These regulations prevented the Jews and Christians from taking any public office, ride horses or camels, or build synagogues or churches higher than mosques. It also forced them to wear distinctive cloth, like a yellow badge. Jews and Christians had to give way to Muslims in the roads; they were banned from giving evidence in a court against a

Muslim and their oath was not accepted in Islamic courts, etc. In today's world, only certain fundamentalist Muslims, the kind of al-Qaida, Hamas, Hizbullah and others, find in the ancient verses of the Quran and passages in the Hadith legitimisation for the use of force, violence or terrorism. The majority of the Muslim people, however, abide with a peaceful interpretation of Islam and consider acts of terror un-Islamic, and those who carry out terror in the name of Islam, pariahs. I think that it mainly depends on the interpretation of Islam by Muslim leaders and on the preaching by Muslim priests. If they are moderate, as the majority of Muslims are, they may perhaps explain the offensive verses as relevant only to the events and people of the times of Muhammad and not to these modern times, but if they are fanatics of the fundamentalist kind, they may regard the verses of the Quran and Hadith immutable and would want to put into practice every verse and passage, verbatim.

The first four Caliphs that succeeded Muhammad were considered "Rightly Guided". Abu Bakr, a close associate of the Prophet and father of his third wife, Aisha, was elected as the first Caliph and chose to be called the "Successor to the Messenger of God", or simply 'Successor' [Caliph]. He died after only two years of reign, and Omer, a close companion of Muhammad and the father of his fourth wife, Hafsa, became the second Caliph in 634 AD. Omer adopted the title: 'Prince of the believers' or 'Commander of the believers' and under his leadership, Islam expanded into Egypt, Syria Mesopotamia, and the Persian Empire was routed. But Omer was assassinated in 644 AD, and Uthman, Muhammad's son in law, took over the caliphate and continued the policy of Islamic conquest until he was also assassinated in 656 AD. After his death, Muhammad's cousin and son in law, Ali, was declared Caliph, but Muawya, the governor of Syria, refused to recognize Ali's succession and demanded an investigation into the murder of Uthman. Muawya and Ali met on the battlefield and fought an inconclusive war. So, they agreed to arbitrate the dispute, but meanwhile Ali was assassinated and Muawya became the fifth Caliph and the first of the Umayyad dynasty that ruled Islam from its capital in Syria from 661 to 750 AD. In that year, a man called Abu al-Abbas; a descendent of Muhammad's uncle, Abbas, usurped the Caliphate by force of arms and exterminated almost all the Umayyad family. He was nicknamed 'Assaffah', which means 'Blood Shedder', for his reign was marked with massacre and terror. His brother moved the capital from Syria to Baghdad, a new city, which he founded in 762 AD.

The Caliphate and the Arab conquests reached their pinnacle during the reign of the famous Caliph Harun al-Rashid and his son Mamun. The nomad Arabs who burst out like a storm from the Arabian Desert to spread Islam over the world, founded a vast empire that encompassed Spain, North Africa, the Middle Eastern countries, Persia and central Asia. Their Capital, Baghdad, was famous for its richness and splendour. Their culture, science and literature were the highest of their time and their civilisation contributed to the development of Europe and the world. Around 770 AD Arab Mathematicians introduced the use of 'zero' in their books and in Europe, although it might have been invented in India earlier; they invented plane and spherical trigonometry; al-Khawarizma invented the logarithms and al-Jabar invented Algebra, both named, with slight distortion, after them; they excelled in astronomical observation and calculated the circumference of the earth within just a minor error of 40 km., centuries before Europe recognized that the earth was not flat; they opened hospitals, universities and libraries; they translated the Greek philosophy to Arabic, and their medical books were used in Europe until the sixteenth century.

The expansion and vastness of the Arab Empire was also the cause of its decline. With the richness and progress acquired, the Arabs had but little motive for fighting and conquests. The Caliphs started to buy slave boys from central Asia and train them as soldiers for their armies. These boys were called 'Mamluks', an Arabic word for 'owned' or 'slaves'. Gradually, the robot turned on his master and the Mamluks, who accepted Islam, became the real rulers. The Caliphs lost the grip of power and the united Empire started to fragment into small independent states, which recognised the position of the Caliph, but only symbolically.

In the middle of the 11th century, between 1040 AD and 1055 AD, the Seljuks, a tribe of primitive Turkmans who grazed the steppes north of the Aral Sea, invaded the Arab Empire and captured Iran and Iraq. Their leader, Togrul Beg, appointed himself protector of the Sunni Caliph of Baghdad and declared war on the Shia'as who had not accepted the Caliph's authority. The Seljuks continued with their expansion, capturing Syria, Palestine and Anatolia and establishing a large empire in the east. Their aggressiveness and desecration of the Holy Sepulchre Church in Jerusalem was the main cause for the launch of the First Crusade in 1095 AD. The division of the Seljuk Empire among younger successors had gradually caused its decline and it was finally defeated and subjugated by the Mongols in 1243 AD.

The Mongols swept from central Asia in the early 13th century like a whirlwind, destroying anything in its way. Their leader, Temujin, whose name was later changed to Genghis Khan [Precious Warlord], was illiterate, but a military genius whose army enjoyed excellent organisation, discipline and manoeuvrability. With his ruthless campaigns and swift invasions he overwhelmed the Middle East, Central Asia, China, and parts of Eastern Europe, like Russia, Poland and Hungary. The Mongol legendary and invincible general Subedei was the first to devise the tactic of 'lightning war', whereby his cavalry carried out swift storming of the enemy's lines, obliterating their defences and throwing them into confusion. The Nazi generals admired the military skills of Subedei; they adopted his tactic and put it to practice in their 'blitz krieg' during the Second World War. The Mongols were the most atrocious invaders; they looted the cities they captured, burned them, killed their men, women and children and made separate pyramids of their skulls. In 1258 they conquered Baghdad, the richest capital of the world, ransacked it, killed its citizens and burned it to the ground, thus bringing to an end the magnificent era of the traditional Caliphate. They were the first to use biological warfare. In 1345 AD, while they were besieging the city of Kaffa on the Black Sea, a dreadful disease, known as the Black Death, swept through their ranks. The Mongol commander ordered his men to catapult the diseased corpses over the city walls. From Kaffa the disease spread to European cities on the Mediterranean, engulfing Germany, Spain and France, and from there, across the Channel, to England and Scandinavia. The Black Death was the greatest disaster in the history of Europe, killing one third of the continent's population.[53]

The Mongols lost their empire in 1368, about the time the Ottomans started to emerge as a new power. 'Othman' was the head of the Turkish tribes that were driven from their homeland in the steppes of Central Asia by the Mongols. The name 'Ottoman' is a slight distortion of his real name. The Ottomans accepted Islam, and settled in Anatolia, the Asian land between the Mediterranean Sea and The Black Sea. They were excellent warriors who established a vast Empire that stretched from the Near East to Europe, capturing Greece and Albania in 1444 and Constantinople, the capital of the Eastern Roman Empire and Byzantium, in 1453. They reached their pinnacle during Sultan Suleiman the Magnificent, but when he died in 1566, the Ottoman Empire started to decline. They remained, though, a formidable power in the international arena until the First World War. Although the Muslim Empire lasted for over 12 centuries, the Arabs, who made the first conquests and established it, ruled for only about 230 years.

8

ANTI-SEMITISM AND ZIONISM

With their emancipation in Western Europe in the late nineteenth and early twentieth centuries, the Jews became more active and often successful in the work they undertook. Their professional and financial success aroused envy among their gentile rivals, which gradually turned into hatred and anti-Semitism. The dislike of the Jews was not something new in Europe, but while the dislike in previous centuries stemmed mainly from religious grudge and hostility by the Christian Church, the new anti-Semitism was caused by jealousy and envy. A good example was the case of Alfred Dreyfus, a Jew who was a Captain in the French Army. He was falsely accused of having given military information to Germany. On 15 October 1894 he was found guilty of espionage and condemned to life imprisonment on the notorious Devil Island. A forged document was later found, the malicious origin of which was concealed by high-ranking officers, but nevertheless he was again pronounced guilty in his second Court Martial, although his sentence was reduced to 10 years imprisonment. Several days later Emile Loubet, the French president, pardoned him.

Dreyfus had served six years of despicable imprisonment for no guilt on his part. Only in 1906 was he fully rehabilitated and restored to the army with the rank of major and decorated with the Legion of Honour.

Among the reporters present in the Dreyfus case, was a young Austrian journalist, Theodore Herzl, who witnessed and reported about the bias and prejudice against the Jewish Captain. Despite being an assimilated Jew, he became very disturbed by the injustice done to the Jewish officer. He heard the mob cries in Paris: 'death to the Jews', and thought that the only solution was to remove the Jews from their hostile surroundings into a country of their own. The Dreyfus case turned Herzl into a fervent Zionist and one of Zionism's most prominent leaders. In 1896, Herzl put his thoughts and ideas down in a pamphlet called 'The Jewish State', unaware that other Jewish leaders in Europe like Moses Hess in Germany, Zevi Kalischer in Poland, Leo Pinsker and Ahad Ha'am in Russia, have already expressed these ideas before him. In 1862, Hess published his book, 'Rome and Jerusalem', and about the same time, Kalischer wrote 'The loving quest of Zion', both books calling for the Jews to establish their homeland in their ancient promised land. The ideas of Hess and Kalischer appealed to Baron Edmond de Rothschild and he organised and financed Jewish agricultural colonies in Palestine. A new movement, 'The lovers of Zion', founded in 1881, organised the immigration of thousands of pioneers to Palestine, establishing many new settlements there.

At first, Herzl sought to solve the Jewish problem in a pragmatic way. In his book 'The Jewish State', he wrote: *"Should the powers declare themselves willing to admit our sovereignty over a neutral piece of land, then the Society will enter negotiations for the possession of this land. Here, two territories come under consideration, Palestine and Argentine".* But after he had realized the strength of the Jewish emotion for their historic homeland, he soon dropped the idea of any 'territory' outside Palestine.

Herzl travelled to the various Jewish communities in Europe, lecturing them on Zionism and gaining many supporters with his charisma and eloquence. In August 1897, he organised a historic conference in Basle where over 200 enthusiastic Jewish leaders attended and passed a resolution to *"create a home in Palestine for the Jewish people, secured by public law".* Herzl believed that the Jewish problem should be dealt with by the international political arena. His aim was to obtain a charter approved by the great powers of the world, granting the Jews a homeland in Palestine. He then went to see the Sultan of Turkey and tried to convince him to allow the Jews to settle in Palestine. He even offered the Sultan an annual fund as a reward, but the Sultan suggested another place in the Middle East. Herzl refused, insisting that Palestine is the only historical homeland of the Jews. After 10 years of intensive work and endeavour to materialize his dream, Herzl died broken hearted in 1904, at the young age of just 44.

Among the audience of Herzl, was a Russian young man by the name of Chaim Weizmann. As a Jew, he could not enrol in a Russian university in his own homeland and therefore went to study in Germany. Weizmann was a devout Zionist with the qualities of a great statesman. He was also a brilliant chemist, with two doctoral degrees in philosophy and science. In 1904 he moved to England as a lecturer in Manchester University, where he befriended the future Prime Minister Arthur James Balfour and was introduced to many influential people and newspapermen. At his laboratory, Weizmann worked out a new method of synthesizing acetone, the material used in high explosives, which proved to be of great help to Britain in the First World War. In gratitude, Balfour and some of his political colleagues reconsidered the question of the Jewish state, and on 2 November 1917, a couple of months before British troops captured Jerusalem from the Turks, the British government issued a declaration. Balfour wrote to Rothschild:

"I have much pleasure in conveying to you, on behalf of his Majesty's Government, the following declaration of sympathy with Jewish Zionist aspirations which has been submitted to, and approved by, the Cabinet. His Majesty's Government view with favour the establishment in Palestine of a national home for the Jewish people, and will use their best endeavours to facilitate the achievement of this object, it being clearly understood that nothing shall be done to prejudice the civil and religious rights of existing non-Jewish communities in Palestine, or the rights and political status enjoyed by Jews in any other country".

The Balfour declaration was the culmination of a long Jewish dream that lasted some 2000 years. It was expressed in their regular prayers in every corner of the Diaspora: *"Next year in Jerusalem as a free people".* However, they would soon find out that it is one thing to declare a homeland for the Jews and another thing to establish it.

Zionism was extracted from the word 'Zion', the name of a mountain in Jerusalem and often mentioned in the Old Testament as a synonym for Jerusalem and the whole of Eretz-Israel. It is a national liberation movement for the return of the

Jewish people to their homeland and the resumption of Jewish sovereignty in the land of Israel.

Since the exile of the Jews from Judea to Babylon over 2500 years ago, and throughout the long centuries of dispersion in the Diaspora, the Jews had not stopped aspiring to return to their historical homeland and live like other nations in freedom and security. There were some disagreements in the Zionist movement, mainly between the Spiritual and Practical streams. There was also a suggestion to settle the Jews somewhere else, but Zionist leaders rejected it off-hand, for the return of the Jews to their ancient land was the heart and soul of their movement.

'Spiritual Zionism' was the ideology of Asher Ginzberg, known by his pseudonym 'Ahad-Ha'am' [one of the people], in which he argued that in 2,000 years of exile, the Jews have lost their creative and national might, and therefore it was imperative to first establish a national spiritual centre of high quality life in Palestine, from which it would radiate to all the Jews in the Diaspora. When this educative activity has succeeded, the right men would rise for the task of establishing a country for themselves. On the other hand, Herzl, and other Jewish leaders of the 'Practical Zionism', believed that the goal should be attained through practical means, such as immigration, agricultural settlement and educational institutions. This movement gained strength in the early years of the twentieth century, and in 1905 a large immigration to Palestine took place, establishing rural settlements, co-opera-tives and new towns. Among the newcomers of this wave of immigration was a young man who arrived from Poland; his name was David Green, later David Ben-Gurion, who became the first Prime Minister of Israel.

Anti-Semitism spread in Germany and France. The term was first coined in 1879 in Germany by an anti-Jewish provoker called Wilhelm Marrih. In France, a nobleman called Joseph Gobineau professed that the French nobility belonged to a 'pure Aryan stock'. The word 'Aryan' normally ascribes to a vast number of Indo-European languages, such as Albanian, Armenian, Celtic, Germanic, Greek, Indo Iranian, Italic, Slavic, Anatolian, etc, but is sometimes used to refer to the people who speak any of these languages. This word was somehow misused by white supremacists who claimed the superiority of certain whites to other people. The term was then narrowed by the Nazis to refer to their 'superior, pure Arian race'. They proclaimed themselves 'the superior race', and the Jews, they claimed, were the inferior race—*"impure, parasites and destroyers"*.

The idea of a 'pure race' is ridiculous, for since the first Homo sapiens came out of Africa, people had been migrating all over the planet, from one site to another, mixing with one another. The Nazi contrivance of a superior and inferior race, is even more ridiculous, for Einstein, according to this theory, belonged to the inferior race, and indeed the Nazi propaganda slighted him and snubbed his theory of General Relativity, saying: *"No one understands it, because there is nothing to understand"*. The Nazis also seized on Darwin's evolution theory, in which the stronger and more efficient survives, while the weaker and less efficient withers and fades away. So, if the weaker and inferior race should be 'helped' to fade away, this would speed up the evolution of the 'superior, pure, Aryan race'.

After the First World War Germany faced great hardships and humiliation. The Germans found in the Jews natural culprits. Hitler, who served as a corporal in the war, accused them of betrayal and of stabbing the German army in the back. Consequently, when Hitler established the National Social Party, Anti-Semitism in Germany became virulent, and incitement against the Jews was the order of the day. The economic crisis and unemployment in Germany after the First World War swayed many young Germans to extremism, with Hitler's party gaining vast support. In 1933, Hitler seized power and became Chancellor of Germany. Jews were now dismissed, not only from governmental posts, but from private firms as well. Intellectuals such as Freud, Einstein and many other scholars, scientists, musicians, playwrights and writers, fled the German hell. In 1935 new laws came into force, stripping Jews of their German citizenship and rights and prohibiting mixed marriages between 'Aryans' and Jews. The incitement soon turned into violence. In November 1938, the Germans burned about 7,500 Jewish shops and 400 synagogues in what was known as the "Crystal Nacht", i.e., the Crystal Night, so called by the Nazis for the glass of the Synagogues and shops' windows that were shattered by the rioters on that night.

The Second World War broke out with the German invasion of Poland in September 1939. In a swift military surge called 'Blitz Krieg', German troops occupied almost all of Europe, and millions of Jews who came under Hitler's control were sent to concentration camps to die of disease and starvation. This was not quick enough for Hitler and in 1942 he devised a diabolical plan to hasten the eradication of Jews. He called it the 'Final Solution', in which massive killing of Jews was carried out in gas chambers. The genocide of the Jews became Hitler's obsession and by the end of the war his murder machine had exterminated six million of the European Jewish population, men, women and children.

In 1975, the UN General Assembly, instigated by a majority of Arab countries, adopted a notorious resolution in which Zionism was equated to racism, although there was nothing spoken, written or done by Zionists that could be considered racist. On the contrary, the Zionists in Palestine wanted to work hand-in-hand with the Arabs in developing the land and building the country. They offered a peaceful hand to the Arabs, but the Arabs rejected it. They did not deprive the Arabs of their rights. They purchased desolate lands, some of which contained swamps and malaria, and paid good money for them. They dried the swamps and developed them into green fields, towns and settlements. The Jews claim their right to rule themselves in their homeland, like any other nation, and Zionism is their national liberation movement. They have never stopped living in Israel and after the Holocaust, when most of the world closed its doors to the camps survivors, many returned to their ancient homeland to find refuge and security. Today, five million Jews live in Israel. They came from over 100 countries, including Europe, USA, the Arab countries, Ethiopia, Sudan, India, Yemen, and many other corners of the Diaspora. Their skin colour is of all shades; black, dark, brown, white and fair. There are also about 1.3 million Arabs, Muslims and Christians, Druze, Baha'is and Circassians, all equal citizens of the Jewish state, as well as foreigners who sought and received citizenship in Israel. On the other hand, some Arab countries practise apartheid against non-Muslims. Jordan, for example, provides citizenship *"to any person who was not Jewish"*, and Saudi Arabia denies citizenship not only to Jews, but also to non-Muslims, and some places are altogether out of bounds for non-Muslims, and yet they were never condemned by the United Nations. However, the hypocritical Resolution against Zionism was revoked by the same United Nations that recklessly adopted it 16 years earlier.

9

ARABS AND JEWS IN PALESTINE

We have briefly discussed the history of the Kingdom of Israel and Judah, the destruction of Jerusalem and the Temple by Titus, and the Jewish revolts of the Maccabeans in 168 BC and of Simon Bar Kochba against the tyranny of Rome in the years 132 to 135 AD. It will be recalled that the last revolt ended with the defeat of the Jews and the literal ploughing of Jerusalem by the Roman troops. Hadrian, the enraged Roman Emperor, punished the rebellious Jews by changing the name of their homeland, from Judea, to 'Philistia'; later becoming 'Falasteen' in Arabic, and 'Palestine' in English.

The Roman Emperor, Constantine, embraced Christianity in 313 AD and his mother, Helena, arrived in Jerusalem as a converted Christian. When she returned to Constantinople, the new capital of the Roman Empire, she brought with her a part of a wooden cross, which she claimed was the cross on which Jesus was crucified. Consequently, the Holy Land attracted hordes of Christian pilgrims, bringing about development and prosperity to this poor part of the Empire. The Byzantine rule over Palestine continued until the Arab invasion, with only a short interruption during its war with Persia, when the latter captured and ruled Palestine between the years 614 and 629 AD. During all this long history of over 16 centuries, from the time of the first Jewish Kingdom in Israel in about 1030 BC until the Arab conquest in 637 AD, the Jewish people formed the preponderant majority in Palestine. During this time, they knew long periods of independence and freedom, and others of occupation and repression. It was only during the Arab and Muslim domination, between 637 and 1099 AD that the number of Jews dwindled to the extent that they became a minority, living as subjugated 'infidels', enjoying spells of tolerance and ill-treatment, alternately.

After the death of Muhammad in 632 AD, the Muslim Arab armies overwhelmed the neighbouring countries, defeating the Persians, the Byzantines in Syria and Palestine and capturing Jerusalem in 638 AD. Contrary to other nations who were given the choice between conversion to Islam or death, the Muslim rulers had normally allowed the 'People of the Book' [the Jews and Christians], to practise their faith, as long as they acknowledged their subordination to the Muslims and adhered to the dhimma (writ of protection) regulations. This, however, was not always the case. We have already mentioned the Muslim Berber sect who captured Spain in 1145 AD and offered the Jews and Christians a choice between conversion to Islam, death or exile. Also, when al-Mahdi captured Khartoum from the small, poorly equipped British-Egyptian force, and killed General Gordon in 1885, he forced all the Jews and Christians to convert to Islam or face death (no other choice was given). There were only eight Jewish families at the time in the Sudan. They all chose to accept Islam rather than die, and the men were forced to marry black, Muslim women, in addition to their white wives, and practise the faith of Islam to the full. It later transpired that the Jews used to say their prayers secretly at home before going to the mosque to show their 'Islamic adherence'. In 1898, General Kitchener recaptured the Sudan from the dervishes of al-Mahdi. The Jews who had converted to Islam returned to their old faith, except for one man, Suleiman Mandeel (probably Mendel, Arabized to Mandeel), a son of a forced convert and a black Muslim mother. The young Mandeel told the rabbi that his black step sisters would not be able to find husbands among the Jews. He remained an ardent Muslim and became a prominent Arab journalist.[57] As a young boy in the Sudan, I used to see a few black Jews, descendants of the other seven families that returned to Judaism. In years to come, some of them immigrated to Israel and have been living there ever since.

In Palestine, however, the Jews and Christians had a better fate. They were allowed to practise their faith and were given some leeway in managing their own community affairs. The Palestinians—Jews and Christians—learned the Arabic language and adopted the Arabic culture, and benefited from the developing trade and commerce that flourished between the Empire's states.

In 687 AD, Caliph Abdel Malik built a magnificent mosque in Jerusalem, the Dome of The Rock. The mosque, which was built in commemoration of the Prophet's Night Journey, stands on the Temple Mount, where the Jewish Temples of King Solomon and Herod the Great once stood. The Muslims believe that this was the site from which the Prophet Muhammad ascended to heaven during his 'Night Journey' to Jerusalem, when he arrived with the angel Gabriel on the back of al-Buraq, the 'horse' whose stride was as far as the eye could see. About two decades later, 'Masjid al-Aqsa', or the Aqsa Mosque, was built on the same site, next to the Dome of the Rock, making the precinct, known as 'al-Haram al-Sharif' [the Noble Sanctuary], sacred to Islam. Thus, apart from being holy for the Jews and the Christians, Jerusalem has now become the third holiest city of Islam, after Mecca and Medina.

It will be recalled that 'Assaffah' [the Blood Shedder] killed the Umayyad Caliph in 750 AD, exterminated his family, and started the Abbasids dynasty. The prosperity that Palestine enjoyed so far ended with the Abbasids and the place became neglected. Palestine went through a long period of unrest and conquests by the Seljuks, the North African Fatimids and the Crusaders. In 1291 AD, the Crusaders lost their last major stronghold, Acre, to the Mamluks and were finally expelled from the Holy Land. The two centuries of the Crusaders Kingdom in Palestine left little mark on the region, except for ruins of castles, fortifications and churches. The traditional Abbasid Caliphate ended with the destruction of Baghdad by the Mongols and the killing of its last puppet Caliph in 1258. However, a symbolic type of Caliphate continued in Cairo until 1516, when the Ottoman Turks defeated the Mamluks in Egypt, conquered most of the countries of the region, including Palestine, and ruled over them for four centuries.

The Crusaders' period in Palestine, from 1099 to 1291 AD, brought with it great persecution and suffering to the Jews and Arabs. However, the Mamluks who expelled the Crusaders and reigned until 1516 AD were tolerant and during their rule many Jews fled persecution in Europe and arrived in Palestine, preferring to live under an Islamic regime, rather than a Christian one. European Jews continued to find a safe haven in Palestine under the long reign of the Ottoman Turks, although they did not always enjoy security, and from time to time they were ill-treated.

The Ottoman Turks divided Palestine into several 'sanjaks' [districts], mostly administered by Palestinians who were appointed by them, answerable to a Turkish pasha-governor in Syria. The attitude to the Jews and Christians changed from time to time, but they were allowed a reasonable measure of autonomy. In good times, they could practise their religion freely and trade with other parts of the Empire. Palestine flourished during the Ottoman peak in the 16th century, but declined in the 17th century together with the Empire's decline. The Jewish population in Palestine waned during the decline of the Ottomans, but started to pick up again from 1882, when Zionist organisations encouraged European Jews to immigrate to the Promised Land.

Palestine in the 19th century was a desolate land, and to a considerable degree empty of population, but Jews have always been living there, mainly in the four holy towns of Jerusalem, Hebron, Tiberias and Safed. While the Jews were a minority in Palestine in the 19th century, Jerusalem has already consisted of a Jewish majority from the first half of that century to today. In 1844 there were 7,120 Jews and 5000 Muslims; in 1896 the number of the Jews in Jerusalem increased to 28,100 as opposed to 8,560 Muslims, and on the breakout of the 1948 War there were 100,000 Jews, compared with only 40,000 Muslims.[35]

During his trip to Palestine in 1867, Mark Twain saw the Jews in these cities and reported about them in a series of letters, written for the "Alta California", a San Francisco paper, about his trip to Europe and the Holy Land. In 1869 he published his best selling book 'The Innocents Abroad', which was mainly composed of these letters. He described the desolation he had seen in Palestine and stated that the total number of inhabitants of Jerusalem amounted to only 14,000 Jews, Muslims, Greeks, and others. About Palestine, he wrote:

"There is not a solitary village throughout its whole extent [the valley of Izrael]—not for 30 miles in either direction. There are two or three small clusters of Bedouin tents, but not a single permanent habitation. One may ride 10 miles hereabouts and not see ten human beings...We travelled some miles of desolate country whose soil is rich enough, but is given over wholly to weeds—a silent mournful expanse...[For] the sort of solitude to make one dreary, come to Galilee....A scene of desolation and misery...the worst I ever saw...hardly a tree or a shrub anywhere [the approaches of Jerusalem], even the olive tree and the cactus, those fast friends of a worthless soil, had almost deserted the country...Jericho is not very picturesque as a ruin. When Joshua ..blew it down..he hardly left enough for the city to cast a shadow...Nazareth is forlorn...Jericho lies a mouldering ruin...Bethlehem and Bethany in their poverty and humiliation....Jerusalem has lost all its ancient grandeur...the wonderful temple which was the pride and the glory of Israel is gone...Palestine sits in sackcloth and ashes...desolate and unlovely...". After his return, he suggested that the title of the expedition should be changed from *"The Grand Holy Land Pleasure Excursion"* to *"The Grand Holy Land Funeral Procession".*[48]

Despite the desolation and scarceness of inhabitants in Palestine, the local and neighbouring Arabs were quite hostile when the Jewish pioneers built up their first settlements and started drying swamps and ploughing the land they had bought.

The Jews brought about work and development with them, creating job prospects for Arabs and improving their economic position, so much so that Arabs from neighbouring countries started to immigrate into Palestine. This, however, did not assuage their hostility and from time to time they raided Jewish settlements, drove the Jews away and usurped their land. The Arabs also requested the Turkish authorities to stop immigration and bar the sale of land to the Jews. Together with the revolt of the Young Turks in 1908, Arab nationalism intensified, inciting hatred against Jews regarding their immigration and settlement in Palestine. Violent riots, however, had not taken place under the daunting Turkish administration, as it later did during the tolerant British mandate.

In the nineteenth century, Arabs living in Palestine identified themselves in terms of their religion. They felt strong bonds with their Muslim brethren in other Arab countries. Those living west of the Jordan directed their allegiance to Damascus, and considered themselves Southern Syrians. The Syrians and the Palestinian Arabs had an aspiration for a Great Syria, encompassing today's Jordan, Syria, Lebanon, Israel and the West Bank, with Emir Faisal of Arabia as its king.

In 1919, after the First World War, when the American President Wilson appointed a commission (the King-Crane Commission) to determine who would act as the mandatory power in Palestine, almost all the Arabs opposed the British and wanted the mandate to be given to America, presuming that the Americans would not implement the Balfour Declaration. The General Syrian Congress, which allegedly represented the Arabs and Jews of Lebanon and Palestine, sent a memorandum to the Commissioners, asking for independence of what they called

Great Syria, demarking its borders and suggesting Emir Faisal of Arabia to be its king. They wrote:

"...absolutely complete political independence for Syria within the boundaries: the Taurus System on the North [mountains chain at southern Turkey]; Rafah and a line running from al-Jauf to the south of the Syrian and Hijazian line to Aqaba on the south; the Euphrates...on the east; and the Mediterranean on the West".

As a young man, the fanatic Palestinian nationalist, Haj Amin al-Husseini, had enthusiastically advocated such affiliation, but when the Syrian aspiration did not materialize and the French, who controlled Syria, refused to accept Emir Faisal Hussein as king of Syria and expelled him in 1920, the Arab leadership of Palestine gradually adopted the idea of independent nationalism and the notorious Hajj Amin al-Husseini soon became the spiritual leader of this new movement.

In December 1917, the British army, under the command of General Edmund Allenby, captured Jerusalem from the Turks. Subsequently, in 1922, The League of Nations agreed on a British Mandate in Palestine. The Mandate's clear purpose was to establish a national home for the Jewish people in Palestine. It stated:

"Whereas the Principal allied Powers have agreed...to entrust to a mandatory selected by the said Powers the administration of the territory of Palestine, which formerly belonged to the Turkish Empire, within such boundaries as may be fixed by them; and.. Whereas the Principal allied Powers have also agreed that the Mandatory should be responsible for putting into effect the declaration originally made on November 2ⁿᵈ, 1917, by the

Government of his Britannic Majesty (the Balfour declaration),
and adopted by the said Powers, in favour of the establishment in
Palestine of a national home for the Jewish people, it being clearly
understood that nothing should be done that might prejudice the
civil and religious rights of the existing non-Jewish communities in
Palestine, or the rights and political status enjoyed by Jews in any
other country; and whereas recognition has thereby been given to
the historical connection of the Jewish people with Palestine and to
the ground for reconstituting their national home in that country".

Article 6 of the Mandate stated that the British
Administration in Palestine shall facilitate Jewish immigration
and encourage settlement of Jews on the land. Hence, it is quite
clear that the League of Nations made Britain responsible for
Palestine in order to facilitate Jewish immigration and establish
a Jewish home in that land.

The traditional territory of Palestine was on both banks of
the River Jordan. In 1921, Britain created on the area east of the
river, which was about 77% of the total area of Palestine, a
kingdom called Trans-Jordan for Prince Abdullah Hussein, as a
reward for the Arabian support and military help to the British
army in defeating and expelling the Turks during World War I.
Shortly thereafter, the British also crowned Abdullah's brother,
Prince Faisal, as king of Iraq. Nevertheless, the Arabian princes
were not satisfied with what they got and claimed that Britain
promised them Palestine as well. That was untrue, for according
to a letter sent to their father, Hussein al-Sharif of Arabia in
1915 by the British high Commissioner in Cairo, Henry
McMahon, on behalf of the Central Government, the British
promised only *"support and independence in territories"* that did

not include areas *"west of Damascus"*. Thus, the whole of Palestine west of the Jordan River was certainly excluded.

The creation of Trans-Jordan aroused much bitterness in both the Jewish and Arab communities of Palestine. The Jews were angry for cutting off such a large chunk of their promised homeland, while for the Arabs it was a further division of 'Great Syria'. The slicing of Palestine continued, and two years later the British ceded the Golan Heights, which was part of Mandate Palestine, to Syria. Jews were prohibited from living or owning property in Trans-Jordan, and those who had been living on the Golan Heights were evacuated and not allowed to live there anymore.

It did not take long after the liberation of Palestine from the Turks before the Arabs started their first riot. It first took place in Jerusalem in March 1920 and was instigated by false and deliberate rumours. Rioters attacked Jews and stabbed several of them to death; they ransacked Jewish homes and set on fire a number of houses; some Jewish women were raped and synagogues and cemeteries were desecrated. Not having prepared an adequate force to tackle such an incident, the British police and army were taken by surprise. They tried to be impartial in dealing with the riots; they arrested Arab rioters as well as some Jews who organized a defensive league. The riots then spread to the north, where Arabs attacked kibbutz Tel-Hay and killed several members of the kibbutz. Lord Balfour was angered by this burst of Arab violence, which, he understood, was an expression of rejection of his 1917 Declaration. In a speech at the Royal Albert Hall on 12 July 1920, he reminded the Arabs that it was Britain who established an independent Arab sovereignty in the Hejaz and were preparing Iraq for self-government. He added:

"I hope that, remembering all that, they will not grudge that small notch—for it is no more than a small notch, that geographically, whatever it may be historically—that small notch in what are now Arab territories being given to the people who, for all these hundreds of years, have been separated from it".[51]

Riots were resumed in 1921 when Arabs attacked Jews in Jaffa and other towns killing 47 and wounding about 140 people. Among those killed was Chaim Brener, the known and admired writer, who was bludgeoned to death while he was trying to escape to Tel-Aviv from his home in Jaffa. A few armed Jews went into Jaffa and retaliated, beating up and killing a number of Arabs. British soldiers intervened to stop the violence and a curfew was announced. The riots were later investigated by the Haycraft Commission that stated: *"The racial strife was begun by the Arabs, and rapidly developed into a conflict of great violence between Arabs and Jews, in which the Arab majority, who were generally the aggressors, inflicted most of the casualties".*

In 1929, due to financial difficulties encountered by the Jewish community in Palestine, the Zionist organisation renewed its financial support. This triggered another Arab riot. The Grand Mufti, Haj Amin al-Husseini, spread false rumours that Jews were planning to take control of holy places. Arab rioters attacked Jews in many settlements and towns, including Jerusalem. 133 Jews and a similar number of Arabs were killed in these riots. The Jews of Hebron, of whom many had been living in this city for over 800 years, bore the main impact of the Arab wrath and a great number of them were massacred by the rioters. Unspeakable atrocities took place there: Jewish babies were beheaded with swords; two elderly rabbis and several young worshippers were castrated; victims' abdomens were slashed open by kitchen knives; some Jews were strangled with ropes; women were raped; Jewish homes, shops and synagogues were ransacked and set on fire. 67 Jews, men, women and children were massacred and scores were wounded in Hebron, among them children that lost both their parents. The British tried to stop the killing and even shot down some Arab rioters, but the few soldiers and Arab policemen were unable to handle that kind of pogrom. It was however not all black in Hebron, for there was another kind of Arab there who risked their lives to save Jews. Most of those who were saved were hidden in Arab homes and without such help, not a Jewish soul would have survived the Hebron Massacre.

Between 1929 and 1938 the Arabs of Palestine conducted a war of terror against the British, the Jews, and Arabs who were accused of collaboration with the 'enemy'. Arab nationalists infiltrated Palestine from neighbouring countries to join the fight against the British and the Jews. The most notorious of these were Izzidin al-Kasam from Syria and Fawzi al-Kawukji from Iraq, who later spent the World War II years in Germany.[39]

In April 1936, the Grand Mufti instigated what became known as the 'Arab Revolt', an insurrection that lasted for about 3 years. The revolt started with a general strike of six months. Its aims were to pressurize the British to halt Jewish immigration, to prohibit the acquisition of Arab land by Jews and to establish an independent Arab state in Palestine. In the first day of the riots 17 Jews were killed, followed by more killing by Arab raiders in Jewish settlements. During this period, the British cooperated with the Hagana, the Jewish

Defence Organisation, both working hand in hand against the terrorists.

In view of the terror and insurrection, the British Government appointed the Peel Royal Commission to investigate a possible solution. The Commission published its report in July 1937. Lord Robert Peel, who headed the Commission, heard a great deal of testimony from both sides of the conflict. In his report, he recommended to abolish the British Mandate and partition the country between the two peoples, allotting a small part to the Jewish state. The Jews reluctantly accepted the partition, but the Arabs responded with another wave of violence. Armed bands attacked British, Jewish and Arab opponents, causing great loss of life and property.

The Central Government responded by sending to Palestine highly competent officers, like Charles Taggart and Bernard Montgomery, to repress the terror. Taggart built scores of fortified police stations all over the mandate area and erected a fence in the northern border to stop the infiltration of terrorists from neighbouring Arab areas; and Montgomery, a professional, pragmatic soldier, who later earned his fame in the battle of Alamein, commanded a whole division for this task. He hit the Arab terrorists with an iron fist, using surprise raids and ruthless retributions. It is estimated that between 1936 and 1940, the British destroyed about 2000 Arab houses in the course of their campaign against the Arab terror. Early in 1939 Montgomery was able to announce that the Arab Revolt was repressed. Between 1936 and 1939, the death toll amounted to 415 Jews and 101 British soldiers. According to an Arab count, about 3,000 Palestinian Arabs were killed in this period.

During the Arab riots, from 1920 to 1939, the British attitude towards the Jews changed from time to time, depending on the Central Government policy, the political situation, the personal leaning of the High Commissioner, the officials and the high ranking officers. The first High Commissioner in Palestine, Herbert Samuel, was a Jewish Zionist who aspired to fulfil the conditions of the mandate regarding a homeland for the Jews, but in face of fierce resistance, he was forced to pacify the Arabs and slow down the immigration of Jews into Palestine. On the other hand, John Chancellor (1928–1931) was pro Arab and tried to influence the Central Government to abandon the Balfour declaration. He was replaced by Arthur Wauchope (1931–1938) who was pro Jewish and believed in the Bible and in the return of the Jews to their historical homeland, as prophesised in the scripture. Harold MacMichael, who took over from him, was neither pro Jewish, nor pro Arab, he was simply pro British, and acted only in the interest of his Administration.[58] But generally, after the 'White Paper' of 1939 that limited Jewish immigration, and the attacks on British life and installations by the Hagana and the Irgun, the British attitude became anti Jewish.

The British had not been successful in carrying out the terms of the Mandate. They neither established a Jewish home, nor did they facilitate Jewish immigration or the settlement of Jews in Palestine. On the contrary, they had impeded both in order to appease the Arabs, whose favour they were keen to gain. They have turned a blind eye to illegal Arab immigration on one hand, and restricted the Jewish Immigration on the other. In 1939, the British knew that the Jews would anyway join them in their impending war against the Nazis, but the Arabs' support had to be won over by wooing and pacification. In breach of the conditions of the mandate, Britain issued a White

Paper limiting the Jewish immigration to only 75,000 immigrants during the following 5 years, after which, the decision was given to the Arabs as to whether to allow more Jewish immigrants into Palestine—a ludicrous option, to say the least.

The Arab riots that started in March 1920 triggered the establishment of the Hagana (Defence), the Jewish defence organisation whose aim was to defend Jewish lives and property. The founders of the organisation had realised that the British army could not be relied upon to protect the Jewish community and decided to establish their own defence force. Young men were recruited, trained, and given military education. They developed new tactics of fighting in the open fields. They aimed to attack armed terrorists only, although that was not always the case and some retaliatory actions were carried out against civilians. Although the British Authorities did not officially recognize the Hagana and considered it an underground resistance, they did perform some joint operations with its members, especially between 1928 and 1938, during the joint fight against the Arab terror. During this period, the Hagana mobilised over 20,000 policemen, field troops, and night squads under the command of Captain Charles Orde Wingate. Wingate was a Christian British intelligence officer who arrived in Mandate Palestine in 1936. He was extremely religious and strongly devoted to the establishment of a Jewish state in Palestine, which he saw as the materialisation of the Biblical prophecy. He trained Jewish young men and formed what was know as the 'Special Night Squads', of Jewish recruits, to carry out military assaults against Arab raiders. Ben-Gurion and other leaders referred to him by the affectionate code name: 'The Friend'. Wingate once said to a Jewish friend:

"I count it as my privilege to fight your battle. To that purpose I want to devote my life. I believe that the very existence of mankind is justified when it is based on the moral foundation of the bible. Whoever dares to lift a hand against you, and your enterprise here, should be fought against".

Moshe Dayan and Yigael Allon, later to become famous generals in the Israeli army, were in their early twenties when they joined the 'Night Squads' of Wingate. Moshe Dayan often mentioned and implemented what he had learned from Wingate regarding the quality and mobility of a force: A small size force, he argued, if well disciplined and trained, can defeat a much larger one. However, this unusual British officer was deported to England when his political opinion and clandestine help to the Hagana were discovered. He was reinstated during the Second World War, fought brilliant battles against the Japanese in Burma and died in an air accident in India in 1944.

The Hagana was under the orders of the Jewish Agency. A group of aggressive members within its lines, however, were angered by the Agency's policy of 'Restraint' towards the Arab violence. In 1932, this group split from the main Hagana force and founded a separate organisation called 'Irgun Tsvai Leumi' (National Military Organisation). At first, it carried out reprisals against Arab bands, but in 1939, with the publication of the White Paper by Britain, the Irgun started terrorist attacks against British targets as well. Menahem Begin, later to be the Prime Minister of Israel, became the leader of the Irgun in 1943. Under his command the Irgun tried to murder the High Commissioner, Harold MacMichael in 1944, but they missed and he was just slightly wounded.

In November 1944 two members of the small terrorist organisation 'Lehi', a splinter of the 'Irgun', murdered Lord Moyne, the British Representative in Cairo, to the great consternation of the Jewish Agency. This terrorist act was strongly condemned by the representatives of the Jewish community in Palestine and the Zionist movement abroad, but its detrimental repercussions were impossible to prevent.

As already mentioned, it was clear to the British since the beginning of 1939, that war with Nazi Germany was inevitable and in haste to pacify the Arabs they halted Jewish immigration. In December 1941, a rickety ship by the name of 'Struma', loaded with Jewish Nazi survivors, was refused permission, both from the British and from the Turkish government, to land. The ship sank as a result of a mysterious explosion, taking with it its 750 passengers, half of whom were women and children. Another sad incident happened with a ship called 'Exodus', the story of which was made into a film in the 1960s. In 1947, the ship, under the command of its 23 years old Hagana Captain Ike Aronovitz (later Arane), stole through the British patrol boats into the gulf of Haifa with 4500 Jewish Holocaust survivors from the displaced persons camps. The refugees refused to be banished from the shore without putting up a fight. In his book 'Personal Witness', Aba Eban described what happened: *"If anyone had ever wanted to know what Churchill meant by 'a squalid war' he would have found out by watching British soldiers using rifle butts, hose pipes and tear gas against the survivors of the death camps".*[10] The British soldiers battled with the holocaust survivors, preventing them to land and forcing them into other ships, to be taken out of Palestinian waters.

During the Second World War about a million Jews fought on the side of the Allies, in addition to about 30,000 volunteers from the Jewish community in Palestine. The policy of the Jewish Agency, as announced by Ben Gurion, was: *"We shall fight the war as if there was no White Paper and fight the White Paper as if there was no war".*[11] The Jewish recruits carried out intelligence and sabotage operations in Vichy Syria and Lebanon, as well as in the Western desert. Moshe Dayan lost his eye during such an operation in Lebanon. Among the volunteers in the British army were many Hagana members who were assigned to combat units where they acquired invaluable military experience as high-ranking officers. Some of these officers were later appointed commanders in Israel Defence Force and fought in the first Israeli Arab war that broke out in 1948.

After the Second World War had come to an end, the plight of the displaced Jewish survivors was unbearable, but the British continued with their anti-immigration policy, blocking the waterway and preventing Jewish immigrants to land in Palestine. The Irgun, as well as the Hagana, intensified their attacks on British targets. The Hagana members freed the interned immigrants from Atlit camp; bombed the country's railroad network; raided radar installations and bases of the British mobile force; sabotaged British vessels that engaged in deporting clandestine immigrants, and in one night destroyed the roads and railroad bridges on the borders, in what became known as 'the night of the bridges'. The Irgun, on the other hand, did not refrain from causing loss of life. They blew up the British Head Quarters at the King David Hotel causing many casualties. They raided and blew up the Acre prison, freeing many underground detainees. They kidnapped and killed English soldiers, after the British Administration had executed three members of their organisation.

The Hagana was engaged not only in operations against the British army, but they also supported the pioneers' movement, helping in the establishment of new settlements, as well as organising their defence and taking part in repelling Arab raiders. The Hagana was also responsible for smuggling illegal Jewish immigrants into Palestine. Under difficult conditions, and in defiance of the British White Paper policy, they succeeded in bringing many thousands of Holocaust survivors into Palestine. When Israel's Independence War broke out, the Hagana became the regular army and without their previous military experience and heroic spirit, it was impossible for the Jews of Palestine to resist the five well-equipped Arab armies that invaded the newborn Jewish state, upon its declaration.

As a result of the Arab revolt and the Jewish underground operations after 1939, the situation became unbearable to the British. Palestine became a millstone round their neck. The financial burden of keeping 100,000 soldiers in a hostile area was enormous, especially as the British economy was almost bankrupt. The pressure of the British public to 'bring the boys home' was great. They therefore elected to withdraw their forces and return the Mandate to the United Nations, the successor of the League of Nations.

In 1947 the United Nations General assembly appointed a Special Committee on Palestine (UNSCOP) to investigate the problem and recommend positive solutions. The Jewish Agency and the Arab High Committee were requested to appoint liaison officers to the Committee. On the Jewish side, Aba Eban was appointed, but the Arabs refused to appoint one. They simply resented the equality with Jews and announced that the British Mandate could be followed by nothing except an Arab

Palestine. This was but one of many grave mistakes made by Arab intransigence.

It was fortunate for the Jewish cause that some of the committee members witnessed the gruesome operation against the refugees of the ship 'Exodus'. Aba Eban, the Jewish liaison officer, later wrote: *"When they came back, they were pale and shocked. I could see that they had come to one conclusion: If this was the only way that the British Mandate could continue, it would be better not to continue it at all"*.[10] The recommendation of UNSCOP was of paramount importance for the Jews, for unless it recommended the establishment of a Jewish State, no country in the United Nations would support such an idea. In September 1947 the Committee published its report. Seven members of the Committee favoured a partition of Palestine between two independent states, an Arab and a Jewish one. A minority of three members favoured a form of cantonization. Despite the small area allotted to the Jewish state, and the internationalisation of Jerusalem, the report was considered good news for the Palestinian Jews. But, the recommendation was just a recommendation, and the final decision was still in the hands of the members of the General Assembly.

The General Assembly was scheduled to vote on the UNSCO recommendation in November 1947. In order for the resolution to be valid, a vote of two thirds of its members was necessary. Jewish representatives at the United Nations carried out tremendous work behind the scenes to persuade members of the Assembly to vote for the Partition recommendation. On the 29th of November, the General Assembly approved the resolution by 33 votes in favour, 13 against, 10 abstentions and 1 absent. Resolution 181 called for the partition of the British-ruled Mandate Palestine into a Jewish state and an Arab state. Among others, the Resolution stated that the United Nations:

"Call upon the inhabitants of Palestine to take such steps as may be necessary on their part to put this plan into effect; Appeals to the Governments and all the peoples to refrain from taking any action which might hamper or delay the carrying out of these recommendations".

The Jews of Palestine accepted the United Nations Resolution 181 with a mixture of glee and concern, while the Arabs rejected it off hand. They proclaimed that *"any line of partition would be a line of fire and blood".*[10]

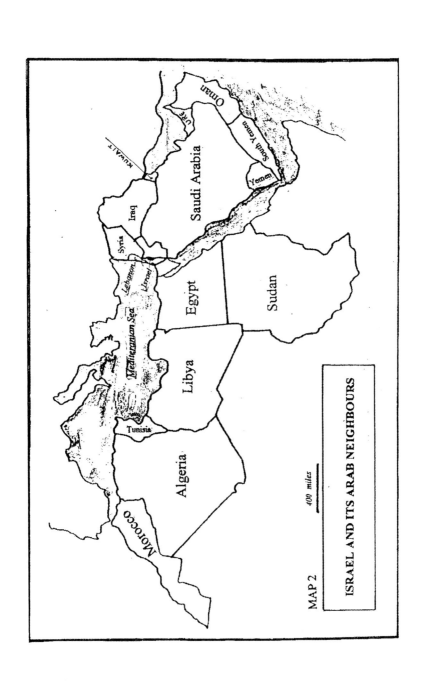

MAP 2

ISRAEL AND ITS ARAB NEIGHBOURS

400 miles

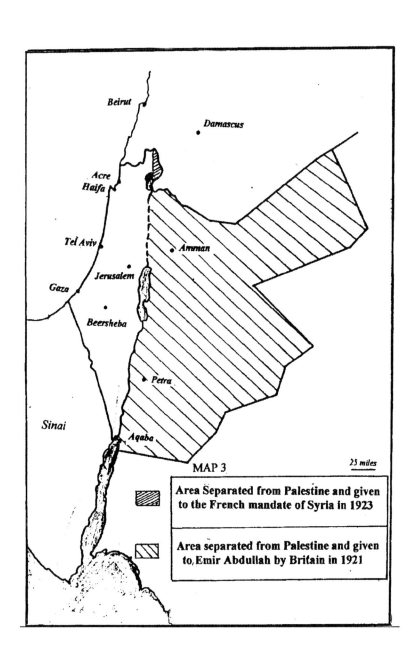

Beirut

Damascus

Acre
Haifa

Tel Aviv

Amman

Jerusalem

Gaza

Beersheba

Petra

Sinai

Aqaba

MAP 3

25 miles

Area Separated from Palestine and given
to the French mandate of Syria in 1923

Area separated from Palestine and given
to, Emir Abdullah by Britain in 1921

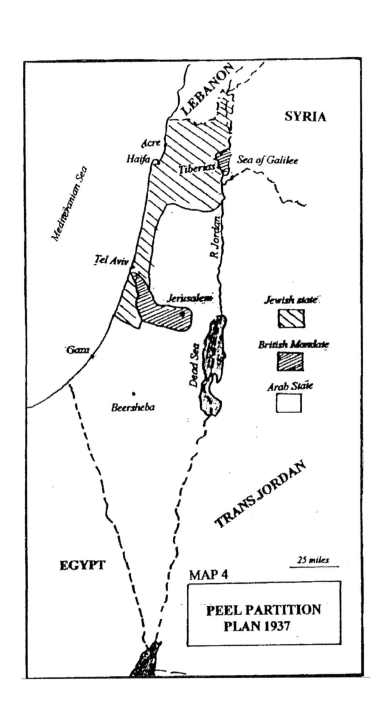

LEBANON

SYRIA

Acre

Haifa

Mediterranean Sea

Tiberias

Sea of Galilee

R. Jordan

Tel Aviv

Jerusalem

Jewish state

British Mandate

Arab State

Gaza

Dead Sea

Beersheba

TRANSJORDAN

25 miles

EGYPT

MAP 4

PEEL PARTITION
PLAN 1937

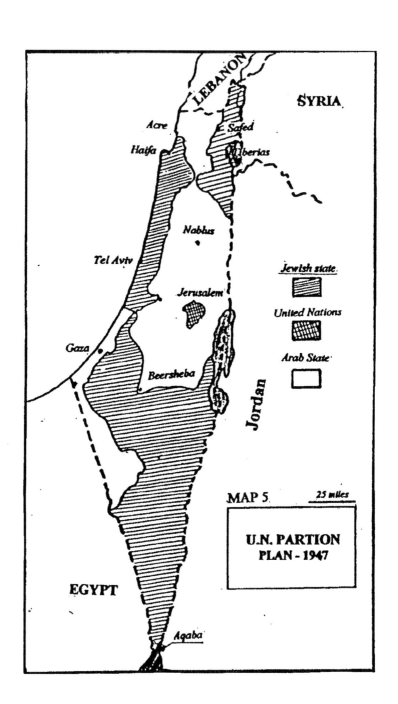

LEBANON

SYRIA

Acre

Safed

Haifa

Tiberias

Nablus

Tel Aviv

Jerusalem

Jewish state

United Nations

Gaza

Arab State

Beersheba

Jordan

MAP 5

25 miles

U.N. PARTION
PLAN - 1947

EGYPT

Aqaba

10

ISRAEL'S WAR OF INDEPENDENCE

When the news of the UN Partition Resolution reached the Arabs of Palestine (they were not known as Palestinians at the time), they responded with a three days strike and intensified their attacks against the Jewish community (the Yishuv). The dominant Arab leader at the time was the Grand Mufti of Jerusalem, Haj Amin al-Husseini. He returned to the area after having aligned himself with Nazi Germany during the Second World War and met with Hitler to discuss the conditions of the Nazi-Arab cooperation and the 'final solution' of the Jews. He visited Auschwitz with Himmler and considered such a death camp for the Jews in Palestine. The Arabs felt quite confident that Germany would win the war and that their interest rested with them. They reckoned that the Nazis and the Arabs were natural allies because they had the same enemies—the Jews, the English and the communists—and as the old adage goes 'the enemy of my enemy is my friend'. During the meeting with Hitler that took place in Berlin on 28 November 1941, al-Husseini offered full Arab cooperation and participation in the war on Germany's side. In return, he wanted a German declaration of support and their help in establishing an Arab legion and eliminating the Jews in Palestine, as well as in other Arab countries. As a grand Mufti, al-Husseini was quite an eloquent speaker. He spoke on Berlin's radio and called upon the Arabs "to kill the Jews…to please Allah". He inflamed his audience with vitriolic speeches, preaching violence and vengeance. Arab militants in Palestine attacked buses, raided settlements and towns, planted car bombs in cities, and massacred scores of fellow Jewish workers in cities composed of Jews and Arabs. They also ambushed convoys with supplies on their way to the various settlements, in what was known as the 'Battle of the Roads', most Palestine's roads running through Arab areas. Having failed to capture Jewish settlements, the Arabs turned to controlling the roads in order to besiege and isolate them. They succeeded in cutting off the road to the Negev that was allotted to the Jewish State by the UN Resolution, and the road to Jerusalem, preventing any supplies or reinforcement to the Jewish part of the capital. March 1948 was a bloody month for the Hagana in which they lost over 100 men in the fight for the roads. However, by finding alternative tortuous ways (like the 'Burma Way' to Jerusalem) and through a series of attacks on Arab strong holds, the 'Battle of the Roads' ended up with the Hagana with the upper hand.

In September 1947 the Arab League was summoned in Lebanon and voted unanimously to prevent the UN Partition Resolution by all means, including military force. The drums of war started beating in the Arab capitals and their leaders proclaimed that they would soon march on Tel-Aviv. The Jewish leadership was faced with a great dilemma. On the one hand there was a historic, legal, international resolution to establish a Jewish state in Palestine, and on the other hand, there were five Arab armies poised on the borders, threatening to prevent the UN resolution by force. There were great pressures and hesitation as to whether to declare Independence and face the risk of annihilation by the Arab forces, or refrain and miss the opportunity that had been awaited for two thousands years. The Hagana was not a regular army. It had fought against Arab bands successfully, but would it be able to resist well-equipped Arab armies? The Jewish National Council was summoned and despite the fear and uncertainty, it took the decision to declare a Jewish state. On 14 May 1948, one day before the departure of the British from Palestine, Ben-Gurion stood up in the Council, the large portrait of Herzl hanging above him, and with a loud and clear voice he read the Declaration of Independence:

"By virtue of the natural and historic right of the Jewish people and the Resolution of the General Assembly of the United Nations, we hereby proclaim the establishment of the Jewish State in Palestine—to be called Israel... With trust in the Almighty God, we set our hands to this declaration at this session of the Provisional State Council in the city of Tel Aviv, on this Sabbath Eve, the fifth day of Iyar, the fourteenth day of May, one thousand Nine Hundred and forty Eight..".

The same day America recognized the new State of Israel, and the Soviet Union's recognition came shortly thereafter. The British were happy to pack up and hand their Mandate back to the United Nations. On 15 May 1948 their troops folded down their flag, boarded their last ship from the port of Haifa and waved goodbye. They left behind a good Administration, well-organised Public Services, and two peoples at the throat of each other. They predicted, and warned, that the Arabs would massacre the Jews soon after their departure. They found it impossible to carry out the terms of the Mandate without using power, which was contrary to their political interest in the Arab world. Palestine for them was a quagmire and they were determined to pull out of it. It was a wise decision. They had no strategic need in Palestine. They suffered loss of life as well as considerable material cost, and had nothing to gain except the hostility and hatred of both the Arabs and the Jews.

No sooner had the Declaration of Independence been read than five Arab armies swarmed across the borders into the land allotted to the Jewish state. Arab leaders proclaimed from their Arab capitals that the Jews would be defeated within days. The Egyptian Army crossed the southern border with an armoured column; the Iraqis advanced from the east; the Arab Legion (Jordan's army) crossed the Jordan River with 'objective Jerusalem'; Syrian tanks, infantry and artillery advanced onto vulnerable kibbutzim in the Jordan valley, while a Lebanese force attacked from the North. Young Israeli soldiers battled with the Syrians and Lebanese in a desperate attempt to stop their advance, or at least delay it. In the eastern front, the Arab Legion besieged Mount Corpus, with its Jewish University and hospital, and in the southern front the Egyptians captured the Iraq-Sheridan fortress in the Negev. To add insult to the Jewish injury, the Egyptian Air Force bombarded Tel-Aviv, killing 42 civilians around the Central Bus Station. This was a day of desperation to the Israelis. A situation of life and death; as Aba Eban later wrote: *"Israel was experiencing the joy of birth and the fear of death in a single taste"*.[46]

On the eve of the Declaration of Independence in May 1948, the total Jewish population in Palestine was about

650,000 and the Arabs about 1,200,000. The Hagana force,
which was transformed into Israel's Army, amounted to 35,300
men and women, and its arsenal included 21,886 rifles, 10,264
sub-machine guns, 1,269 machine guns, 682-2 inch mortars,
105-3 inch mortars and 25 artillery pieces.[11] Against this force
stood the Arab armies with a total of 150,000 men. Egypt Air
Force had 177 fighters and bombers and the Arab Legion had
50 heavy guns and 400 tanks.[12] In addition, there were the
Syrian, Lebanese and Iraqi troops. To Israel it was the battle of
David against Goliath.

After 10 desperate days of fierce fighting on three fronts,
Israel received the first batch of Messerschmitt fighters that
arrived from Czechoslovakia, as well as a ship with armament,
including 45 heavy guns, which were purchased in Europe
before the start of the war. *"This was the turning point"* said Ben-
Gurion later. But even prior to that, the Syrian tanks were
repelled or destroyed by Molotov Bottles at the gates of kibbutz
Deganya, the advance of the Lebanese and Egyptians was
blocked and the Iraqis who threatened to cut Israel in two, were
stopped at Jenin, never to resume their advance westwards
again. A black cloud of annihilation was removed from the skies
of the Jewish State, and when a four-week armistice was agreed
on 11 June 1948, the Israeli army was in control, not only of
the land allotted to Israel by the Partition Resolution, but of
other areas beyond the demarcation line. Albeit, the Jewish
quarter in Jerusalem had fallen to the Arab Legion and was to
remain in their hands for the next 19 years.

The ceasefire was needed by Israel like rain on arid land. The
army was re-organised in this short period. Immigrants, who in
the meantime landed in Israel, were trained and absorbed in
various combat units; large amounts of armament, including

fighters and bombers were received from abroad and absorbed by the Israeli army. The fighting was resumed by the Egyptians 28 hours before the official elapse of the ceasefire, but now the Israeli army was a different force, and as the Head of Operations, Yigael Yadin, later said: *"After the Ceasefire, the initiative passed to our hands and we never gave it back to the Arab forces".*[12]

The second round of fighting lasted only 10 days, but brought significant territorial gains to the Israelis. However, the Arab Legion, the best trained force in the Arab world, which had been under the command of the experienced British officer Sir John Bagot Glob since 1939, stood firm in the old city of Jerusalem and held the fortress of Latrun that controlled the main road to Jerusalem, despite repeated attacks by the Israelis. The second armistice came into force too soon for the Israelis, as the Egyptians were still in control of the Negev. Ben-Gurion was anxious to liberate the Negev that was part of the allotted Jewish State. He devised a convoy with supplies to a locked-up Jewish post in the Negev, anticipating the Egyptians attacking it, and thus breach the terms of the armistice. Indeed, the Egyptians fell into the trap, attacked the convoy and put two trucks on fire under the watchful eye of the UN Surveyors. The Israeli army, as planned beforehand, opened with a frontal attack. The Egyptians fought boldly and stubbornly, but retreated when they realized that Israeli troops were about to surround them. The battles for the Negev were the fiercest that the Israeli army knew in that war, but when another ceasefire came into force on 20 October 1948, the Negev, including its capital, Beer Sheba, were in Israeli hands. One single Egyptian pocket, at Faluja, remained besieged and fought with great valour. Among the Egyptian fighters, there was a young officer by the name of Gamal Abdel Nasser, later to be the president of Egypt, who instigated the Suez Canal war in 1956 and started the Six-Day War in 1967. Faluja was eventually evacuated peacefully with the final armistice agreement with Egypt.

The war with Egypt was not without an intriguing episode. During the Israeli attack in the Negev, Israeli troops penetrated the international border and captured several positions in Sinai. Britain warned Israel to evacuate the captured territories immediately, or otherwise they would have to interfere in accordance with their defence pact with Egypt. A few Spitfire aircraft were dispatched over the Israeli troops to prod their withdrawal. Israeli pilots brought down three of them. Several hours later, another two Spitfires were shot down. One of the Israeli pilots engaged in the dogfight was Ezer Weizmann, later to be the president of Israel. When the news about the clash with British aircraft reached Ben-Gurion, he jittered, and immediately ordered the army to withdraw from Sinai.

In February 1949 an armistice was agreed with Egypt, in March with Lebanon and in April with Jordan. The Syrians finally agreed to sign a ceasefire agreement in July, and the Iraqis have never signed an agreement to date. Thus, the Independence War came to an end. Israel was victorious, but the price it paid in human life was tremendous. Over 6,000 killed and 15,000 wounded. In American scale, this was equivalent to 1.6 million killed and 4 million wounded. Jordan captured and annexed the West Bank and East Jerusalem, including the Old Jewish Quarter, and controlled their Palestinian population, and Egypt did the same in the Gaza Strip, though without officially annexing it. The war thus ended with Jewish victory. Their improvised army defeated 5 regular Arab armies, because its soldiers had a much greater motivation to defend their homes and families against those who threatened to slaughter and "throw them to the sea", while the Arab armies were fighting a war of aggression on a foreign land, far from their homes and loved ones.

Hundreds of thousands of Arab refugees left their homes and fled to the Gaza Strip, the West Bank and other Arab territories. The exact number will never be known, but it was estimated at about 500,000 to 700,000, with the UN Mediator reporting a figure of 472,000, of whom only about 360,000 required aid.[42] What caused so many Arabs to flee their homes? Mainly fear and panic, which the incident of 'Dir Yassin' may have contributed to, although many Arabs fled before Dir Yassin. They were confident that they would return soon "after the Arabs have won the war". Many left their homes because they were told to do so, "temporarily", in order to clear the way for the Arab armies until the Jews have been defeated. In addition, there were instructions by the Arab High Commission, forbidding them to sign a surrender agreement, which caused them to prefer escape to surrender. Dir Yassin was a small village near Jerusalem. On 9 April 1948, members of the Irgun and Lehi (a splinter of Irgun) approached the Arab village in order to attack it. They used loudspeakers to warn the villagers, but the Arabs did not run away, on the contrary, they put up a fierce fight. The battle went on for many hours, but when the fire died out, the raiders were said to have massacred those who fell into their hands. It was later alleged that the blood bath was not premeditated, but the fierce Arab resistance, and the loss of comrades, turned the raiders' fury into a violent hysteria. About 200 men, women and children were said to have been killed in the course of the battle and the ensuing massacre. So it was believed for many years until 1987 when a group of Palestinian scholars from the University of Bir Zeit researched the subject and concluded that the number of casualties did not exceed 120. A survivor of the massacre later confirmed this number. In his book 'Holy Land Unholy War', the author, Anton Laguardia, a veteran journalist who spent many years in Jerusalem as the Daily Telegraph's reporter, stated that he interviewed a 65 year old survivor of Dir Yassin, Ayish Zeidan, who testified that he never believed that more than 110 people had died at Dir Yassin and that most of those who were killed were among the fighters and the women and children who helped the fighters.[13] It could well have been that the exaggerated number of 200 was falsely claimed by both sides, the one to arouse the fury of their people and inflame them to revenge and vengeance, and the other to frighten the Arabs and make them flee. Whether 200, 110 or 10 victims, some kind of massacre had taken place in Dir Yassin and has since become a blot on the escutcheon of Israel.

As the news of the massacre spread, the Jewish community and their leaders were appalled at the atrocity committed by the dissident revisionist groups, and they strongly condemned it. They even sent a telegram to king Abdullah of Jordan, expressing deep regret and shock. The Arabs, however, did not wait long to take their revenge. A few days later, they ambushed a convoy on its way to the Jewish University and the Hadassa Hospital on Mount Corpus; 70 Jews were burned alive in the fire attack, among them were well known doctors, nurses and University staff.[12] Ben-Gurion now became more determined than ever to disband the dissident organisations of the Irgun and Lehi. Two months after Dir Yassin, he used military force and suppressed the last vestige of dissension, not without the cost of Jewish lives lost in the course of the fire exchange.

Interestingly, however, this one atrocity of Dir Yassin, committed by a dissident Jewish militant organisation, was engraved as a black stain in the history of Israel, while many similar, or worse, atrocities committed by Arabs against Jews, did not seem to leave any similar mark on the Arabs. It is as if they are being excused for their atrocities, while the world expects a higher degree of humanity from the Jews.

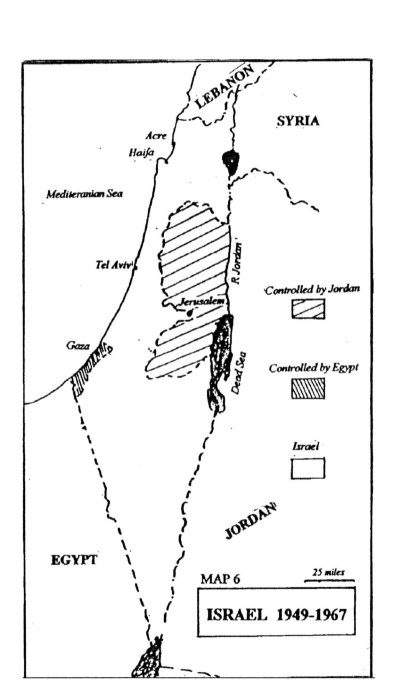

LEBANON

SYRIA

Acre

Haifa

Mediteranian Sea

Tel Aviv

R. Jordan

Jerusalem

Gaza

Dead Sea

Controlled by Jordan

Controlled by Egypt

Israel

JORDAN

EGYPT

MAP 6

25 miles

ISRAEL 1949-1967

11

THE SINAI CAMPAIGN

After the war, hundreds of thousands of refugees landed in Israel, wave after wave. Many of them were camps' survivors, but a great number were Jewish refugees from Arab countries, who had been expelled and their homes and property confiscated. Israel was faced with awesome challenges. The newborn state, with a population of just 650,000, was plunged into enormous difficulties of housing and feeding such great numbers of refugees. But while it was grappling with its economic crisis, immigration absorption and security needs, its neighbouring Arab states had been training terrorist groups and encouraging them to penetrate Israel for acts of murder and destruction. Egypt and Syria were the main instigators and supporters of such actions. They opened training camps in the Gaza strip and Syria and provided the terrorists with arms and intelligence information. The 'Fedayeen' (sacrificers), as those terrorists were called, carried out audacious operations deep inside Israeli territory. In the evening of 24 March 1955, a group of 'Fedayeen' approached under the cover of dark a house in the village of Patish, where a wedding party was taking place. They attacked the revellers with automatic guns and grenades, leaving behind 22 killed and wounded. This was just one of many and continuous terrorist attacks that originated from the Gaza strip, Syria and Jordan, with the knowledge, aid and encouragement of the Egyptian and Syrian authorities (terrorists that arrived from Jordan had normally originated from Syria). Between 1951 and 1955, over 500 Israelis were killed as a result of terrorist attacks from Jordan, over 400 killed by attacks from Egypt and about 60 by attacks that originated from Syria.

Israel though did not sit like a lame duck during this terrorist campaign. Ariel Sharon was a young major in the Israel Defence Force when he was given command of the redoubtable commando 'Unit 101', which carried out reprisal actions inside the Arab countries from which the terrorists came. In October 1953, a most unfortunate operation was carried out in the Jordanian village of Kibya in retaliation of the murder of a mother and her two children. When the Force approached the village, the Arab residents started fleeing. Israeli sappers blew up several dozens of houses, not knowing that some residents were hiding inside them. 69 men, women and children were killed in the blasts and the disaster shocked the whole world, the Arabs and the Israeli public alike. As a result of Kibya, the Head of Operations, Moshe Dayan, issued clear orders that only military targets should be attacked in the future.

In September 1955, Egypt's president, Gamal Abdel-Nasser, closed the air space to Israeli planes above the international waterway of the Tiran Straits. This arbitrary action was carried out suddenly and without any provocation. The port of Eilat became useless and El-Al was forced to cancel its flights to South Africa. Shortly thereafter Israel's concerns reached an alarming point when Nasser disclosed a large armament acquisition from Czechoslovakia, a Russian satellite at the time.

The large amounts of armament included, among others, 200 Mig15 fighter aircraft and Illusion bombers, 230 tanks, mobile guns, destroyers and submarines. Israel, at the time, had only 30 fighter aircraft and no bombing planes at all. The Egyptian media became more and more bellicose. Cairo Radio proclaimed: *"there will be no peace at the borders, because we want revenge, and revenge means death to Israel"*. The United States refused to supply Israel with the necessary arms to ward off the Egyptian threat. France on the other hand was responsive. Prime Minister Guy Mollet, who was eager to punish Nasser for his support and help to the Arab rebels in Algeria, agreed to provide Israel with 72 Mister-4 fighter aircraft and 200 light AMX tanks.

On 26 July 1956, Nasser, in a dramatic speech in Alexandria, announced the Naturalisation of the Suez Canal. This aggressive act infuriated Britain and France (the shareholders of the Canal) and created a strong cause for them to collude with Israel on a joint attack on Egypt. The three 'partners' of the collusion had a common, but different interest. Israel wanted to put an end to the terrorist attacks against its citizens, and France and England wanted to regain control of 'their' Canal. In accordance with the secret plan, Israel captured the Gaza strip and advanced into Sinai, reaching 10 km from the Suez Canal as previously agreed with the two allies. Subsequently, England and France issued an ultimatum to the warring sides to withdraw from the Canal, and when the Egyptians refused, the two 'Powers' started a bombardment on strategic areas along the Suez Canal, followed by a parachute landing to recapture it. In one week, the Israeli forces captured the Gaza strip and the Sinai Peninsula, reopening the Tiran Straits for free navigation. The British and the French on the other hand had less success and their paratroopers were being bogged down in unsuccessful fighting with the Egyptians, with no sign of victory on the horizon.

The Americans, who were not brought into the secret of the joint attack on Egypt, were furious. They applied immense pressure, demanding the immediate withdrawal of England, France and Israel from Egyptian territory. Russia went even further, threatening France and Britain with nuclear war and Israel with its very existence. Ben-Gurion read the Soviet warning and retorted: *"Had the message of Bulganin not borne his signature, I would have thought it was written by Hitler".*[12] France and Britain were forced, under the immense pressure by the two superpowers, to withdraw from Egypt without securing any gains. On the other hand, Israel put up a fierce resistance, arguing about the terrorist attacks, its border's security and freedom of navigation on the international waterway. Finally, Israel withdrew its forces, but not before obtaining a commitment from the United States, Britain and France, to maintain the Tiran Straits open to Israel for free navigation. As will be seen in the following chapter, this commitment was later put to the test and proved utterly useless.

In the short term however, the Sinai campaign was beneficial to Israel. It brought about 10 years of peace, with total quiet on its borders. UN troops were placed on the Sinai border, in the Gaza strip and at the Tiran Straits, which were reopened to Israeli ships. The port of Eilat, now open to world navigation, expanded and the city flourished as a centre of tourism. At least, Israel knew ten years of security and prosperity, before the cloud of war darkened again amid the summer of 1967.

12

THE SIX-DAY WAR

In its effort to gain influence in the Middle East, the Soviet Union decided in 1953 to abandon its support of Israel and champion the Arab cause. After the Suez-Sinai Campaign, the Russians began pouring huge amounts of armament into Arab countries, such as Egypt, Syria and Iraq, while the United States was still refusing to arm Israel. Aba Eban, Israel's Ambassador to America, who was not given admission to the White House on this matter, voiced Israel's concerns on a CBS Newscast. He argued that the Americans were supplying tanks to Saudi Arabia; the British supplying planes and tanks to Iraq; the Soviet Union bombers, fighters, tanks and submarines to Egypt, and Israel receives no means to defend itself against its hostile neighbours, *"what kind of policy is that?"* he asked.[10] At this dire time however, France came to Israel's aid and supplied it with the armament required for its defence.

In 1962, the Israeli foreign Minister, Golda Meir, addressed the Arab states at the United Nations General Assembly suggesting *"complete disarmament with mutual inspection, covering all types of weapons… "*, but the Arabs snubbed the offer. They felt militarily confident after having received large amounts of armament from Russia. Consequently, Syria renewed terrorist infiltrations and sabotage attacks inside Israel. In April 1967, after a series of border clashes and fire exchanges with the Syrians, a number of Mirage fighters were sent to silence the fire sources on the Golan Heights. Syrian fighter aircraft intercepted the Israeli pilots, and in the course of the dogfight six Syrian planes were shot down. This incident augured well for the Russian intention to inflame the already precarious situation. They falsely informed Egypt and Syria that Israel was concentrating large forces on the Syrian border. On 15 May 1967, while Israel was celebrating its Independence Day, the Egyptian army suddenly crossed the Suez Canal on its way to the Israeli border. Nasser expelled the UN troops from all Egyptian territories, closed the Tiran Straits to Israeli navigation and proclaimed that the liberation of Palestine was near. Nasser explained his actions:

"On May 13", he said, *"we received accurate information that Israel was concentrating on the Syrian border huge armed forces, about 11 to 13 brigades…The decision made by Israel at the time was to carry out an attack on Syria, starting on May 17. On May 14 we took action and discussed the matter with our Syrian brothers".*

In fact there were no Israeli force concentrations at the Syrian border, or at any other border, nor was there any Israeli intention to attack Syria. Subsequently, the Russian Ambassador brought, personally, a warning message to the Israeli Prime Minister, Eshkol, in the middle of the night. It was from the Russian President, accusing Israel of belligerence and threatening it with dire consequences. Eshkol challenged the ambassador to take his military attaché to the Northern border and find out for himself whether there were any Israeli forces there, but the Ambassador answered that his function was *"to communicate Soviet truth, not to put it to the test".[10]*

The Arab leaders, as well as the Arab media, poured oil on the fire. The inflamed mob burst into the streets of the Arab capitals shouting war slogans and hailing Nasser as the hero of the Arab people and the liberator of Palestine. Buoyed by the support and admiration of millions, Nasser spoke on 23 May 1967 to officers at an air base in Sinai and said:

"Our armed forces have occupied Sharm-El-Sheikh [Tiran Straights]. We shall under no circumstances allow the Israeli flag to pass. The Jews threaten with war, and I say to them 'Ahlan wasahlan' [welcome], we are ready, and our basic objective will be the destruction of Israel".[52]

Israel was in a desperate situation. There was no point in summoning the UN Security Council, for the Soviets, Arabs, and their cronies, dominated the Council. On the contrary, it may even tie Israel's hands to take any necessary action. England and France reneged on their commitment from 1957 to maintain the Tiran Straits free for all nations. The Americans, who were a party in promising Israel free navigation after the Sinai Campaign, tried to organize an international force to open the waterway, but their efforts were sterile and they were forced to abandon the idea. After three weeks of alarm and anxiety, Israel realized that the Western Powers were not prepared to take any action. With the large Arab forces of Egypt, Saudi Arabia, Jordan and Syria poised for battle at its Southern, Eastern and Northern borders, and with Nasser threatening to destroy it, Israel had no other choice but to fight for its very existence.

On the early morning of the 5th June 1967, Israeli pilots struck against the airfields of Egypt and Syria, destroying most of their aircraft. At the same time a three-pronged ground attack of tanks and infantry was launched on the Gaza strip and into the Sinai Peninsula. As to Jordan, the Israeli Cabinet decided not attack Jordan unless it attacked first. The UN Chief of Staff, General Odd Bull, was asked to pass a message to King Hussein, that if Jordan did not interfere, it would suffer no harm. But instead, Hussein started bombarding the Jewish part of Jerusalem. King Hussein admitted later that although he had received the Israeli message, it had arrived when his forces were already fighting in Jerusalem and his planes had started bombarding Israeli air bases. His answer to Odd Bull was quite terse: *"They started the battle; well, they are receiving our reply now".*[14] Hussein's confident reply was understandable in view of the facts mentioned in his book, 'My War with Israel'. He wrote that the Egyptians had deceived him by falsely informing him that they had destroyed 75% of Israel's Air Force, started a counter attack over Israel, and that their troops in Sinai had taken the offensive on the ground. He added that the false Egyptian reports confused the Jordanians and caused them to misread the map of the war and misinterpret the situation. To such a degree was the Jordanian confusion, that when they saw planes on their radar, flying from Egypt towards Israel, they believed that they were bombers of the Egyptian Air Force, on their way to carry out a mission over Israel. *"They were not"*, he said, *"they were Israeli planes returning home after having accomplished their mission".*[14]

Israel was now at war with three Arab countries. The war with Egypt was going well for the Israelis and taking place far from its population centres. The Syrians were meantime held at bay at the Golan Heights, but the Jordanian's bombardment on Jerusalem was causing loss of life and severe damage to property. The Jordanians had also captured the strategically important UN building (the ex British High Commissioner's palace) in Jerusalem, and surrounded Mount Corpus, with its Jewish hospital and University. Orders were consequently given to the Israeli army to counter-attack. Fierce battles took place in the streets of the Old city of Jerusalem and around the Jordanian fortified trenches. The Jordanians fought with great courage, but after a bloody and lengthy battle, they were defeated. Israeli troops moved with relative ease through the West Bank, reaching the Jordan River. The whole West Bank was now in their hands.

In four days, Israeli troops swept through the Gaza Strip and Sinai, taking control of the whole peninsula and ending up on the East Bank of the Suez Canal. The devastation of the Egyptian army was complete. Their Air Force was extinct, many hundreds of their tanks were either demolished or captured, thousands of soldiers lost their lives and many other thousands were taken prisoners. On the Northern front, the Syrians were well dug-in into fortified trenches on the Golan Heights. The terrain was very difficult for the Israeli soldiers who were making their way uphill to attack the Syrian positions. After two days of fierce fighting, the Syrian army collapsed, and the Golan Heights fell into Israeli hands. Losses were heavy on both sides: 115 Israeli soldiers lost their lives and 320 were wounded, while the Syrians suffered 1000 dead and some few thousand wounded.

The war ended with an entertaining episode, which became known in the West as 'The Big Lie'. In a radio broadcast on 9 June 1967 Nasser announced his resignation, just to withdraw it again the following day, under "public pressure". In his broadcast address, Nasser contrived a story to excuse his army's defeat and alleviate the Arab humiliation. He said:

"It had been established that American and British aircraft carriers were off the shores of the enemy helping his war effort. Also, British aircraft raided, in broad daylight, positions on the Syrian and Egyptian fronts, in addition to operations by a number of American aircraft reconnoitring some of our positions. The inevitable result of this was that our land forces, fighting most violent and brave battles in the open desert, found themselves...without air cover...Indeed, it can be said without emotion or exaggeration that the enemy was operating with an air force three times stronger than his normal force".[52]

This lie had previously been concocted with Jordan. Before his resignation address, Nasser called King Hussein, suggesting, in an open telephone conversation, to issue false statements saying that British and American forces were involved in the fighting on Israel's side. Such a revelation, Nasser thought, would be a great consolation to the Arab people, for it would be more acceptable to be defeated by great powers than by the 'disdained Jews'. Unfortunately for him, the Israelis tapped the conversation and repeatedly broadcast it to the whole world.

In the aftermath of the fighting, the Russians demanded Israel's immediate withdrawal to the borders that existed on June 4th, plus a UN resolution condemning Israel for 'its aggression'. In turn, Aba Eban spoke in the United Nations and said that the war with the Arab states had many consequences but only one cause: *"Israel's right to peace, serenity, sovereignty, economic development, and marine freedom"*. He mentioned the incessant threats and attacks on the Jewish state and the Arabs' determination to deny Israel the right to exist.

Israel offered peace to its Arab neighbours, suggesting slight border modification. The June 4th borders, Israel argued, were irrational in some places, and had to be modified in order to diminish temptation for future aggression. These proposals were scornfully rejected by the Arab states. Instead, the Arab League met at a conference in Khartoum, and on 1 September 1967, at the behest of the Egyptian President Nasser, it took a resolution known as 'the three NOs Resolution'; i.e. No Negotiations; No Recognition; and No Peace with Israel. The General Assembly rejected the Russian-Arab proposal to condemn Israel for its pre-emptive action, or force it to withdraw without peace negotiations. Finally, a UN Resolution no. 242 was formulated by the United Kingdom. It called upon Israel to withdraw from 'occupied territories'. It did not call for the withdrawal from 'all the territories', and not from 'the territories', but from 'territories'. George Brown, the British Foreign Secretary at the time, stated in his book, 'In My Way', that Britain took over the drafting of the resolution (242) after all other delegates failed in wording a proposal that would be acceptable to the warring parties. Lord Caradon (Hugh Foot), who was the British Minister at the United Nations at the time, took upon himself the *"impossible task"* and did an *"absolutely monumental job"*.[15] The resolution proposed was carefully balanced and specified what the Israelis and the Arabs would have to do in order to secure peace in the Middle East and the recognition of the State of Israel. The resolution therefore called for the withdrawal of Israeli armed forces from territories occupied in the recent conflict and also for the termination of belligerence between all states. George Brown also stated in his book that the resolution did not call for Israel to withdraw from 'the' territories recently occupied, nor did it use the word 'all'.[15] *"In order to achieve peace"*, he said, *"each side must be prepared to give something"*.[15]

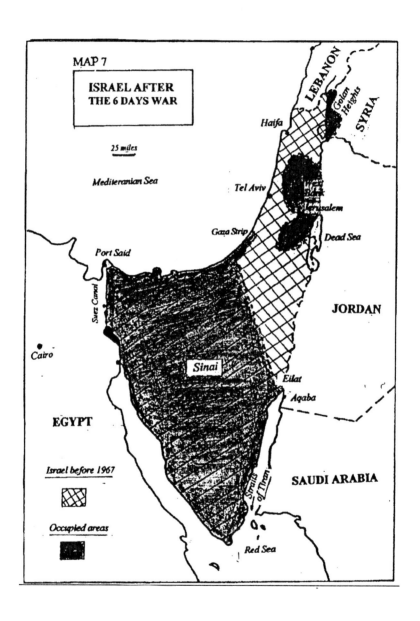

MAP 7

**ISRAEL AFTER
THE 6 DAYS WAR**

25 miles

Mediteranian Sea

LEBANON

Golan Heights

SYRIA

Haifa

Tel Aviv

Jerusalem

Gaza Strip

Dead Sea

Port Said

Suez Canal

JORDAN

Cairo

Sinai

Eilat

Aqaba

EGYPT

Israel before 1967

Occupied areas

SAUDI ARABIA

Straits of Tiran

Red Sea

13

YOM KIPPUR WAR

Since the end of the Six-Day War, Israel had been trying through various intermediaries to arrange peace talks with the Arab States, and particularly with Egypt. While Nasser adhered to the three famous NOs of the Khartoum Conference, clandestine talks took place with King Hussein, but without any significant results. In 1969 Nasser started a war of attrition against Israel along the Suez Canal, but having achieved nothing except heavy losses on both sides, he agreed to a ceasefire in 1970. In September the same year Nasser died of a heart attack and was succeeded by Anwar Sadat. Through secret diplomatic channels, Sadat indicated that he would agree to sign a peace agreement with Israel, if it would withdraw from all territories captured in 1967. Israel's understanding of Resolution 242 was that certain borders could be modified, but Sadat demanded full withdrawal from 'all the areas', and not only from 'areas' as stated in the UN Resolution. Consequently, Egypt and Syria started preparing for war. Knowing that they could not defeat the Israeli army in straight confrontation, Egypt and Syria devised a ploy. In September 1973, Egypt concentrated large forces on the West Bank of the Suez Canal, while the Syrian army took positions on the northern border.

The Egyptians pretended to be carrying out regular manoeuvres, and the Syrians claimed that they were just taking precautions against a possible Israeli attack. The Israeli assessment of the situation was that the probability of war was low. It was thought that the Arab armies, knowing Israel's absolute command in the air, would not risk an attack and expose their forces. Another reason for this wrong appraisal was that a similar Egyptian concentration of forces took place in May the same year. In that case, the Israeli army took every necessary precaution and mobilized a large number of reservists, whereupon the Egyptian forces dispersed without a shot being fired. Mobilizing the reserve forces was an exercise that cost the Israeli taxpayer many millions of shekels. It is believed that the memory of what had happened in May played a major role in the Israeli misinterpretation of the real Arab intentions during the events of September 1973.

In the early hours of 6 October it became clear to the Israeli Intelligence that the two Arab armies would simultaneously start war against Israel sometime before sunset. The Chief of Staff suggested a pre-emptive strike, but it was rejected on political grounds. It is significant that the Egyptians chose Yom Kippur, the holiest day in the Jewish calendar, for their attack. The Arab World had often been sensitive about any military action during their Islamic feasts, and the vociferous protests of the Muslim countries against the United States' bombardment in Afghanistan during their fasting feast of Ramadan was a recent example. This rule, however, seems to hold only when Muslims are attacked, not when they do the attacking, for they started the war not only on the holiest Jewish feast, but also on their own holy feast of Ramadan.

In every Yom Kippur, the atonement and holiest day of the Jewish calendar, Israel literally comes to a halt; no cinemas, television or radio transmissions; no restaurants or coffee shops; no buses or trains, or even private cars are seen on the roads. In this sense, the choice of Yom Kippur was quite helpful to Israel, because it was much easier to locate the reservists who were either at home or in the Synagogue. Also, transporting the reservists to their units was made much more quickly, with all the roads free of traffic jams.

The Egyptians crossed the Suez Canal by pontoons, boats and bridges and captured the thinly manned Israeli positions on the East Bank. By dusk, the Egyptians were in control of the East Bank with 80,000 soldiers and 1,000 tanks. On the northern front, the Syrians advanced with 40,000 men and 800 tanks, capturing the Golan Heights. The first day of the war was a black day for Israel, with heavy losses in men, aircraft and tanks. The Israeli army became inhibited and could not launch a counter-attack, and it was necessary to ask the United States for quick replacement of the lost equipment. Nixon, the American president, knew that an Israeli defeat by Soviet weapons would be a political disaster to America. He ordered the Defence Department to send to Israel, as soon as possible, Galaxy aircraft with the necessary armament. Meanwhile, Ariel Sharon, a daring Israeli General, led his paratroopers through a seam between the Second and Third Egyptian armies, crossed the Suez Canal on pontoon barges, and established a bridgehead on its West Bank. A floating bridge was then erected and Israeli tanks and troops poured over it westwards, pushing forward to encircle the two Egyptian armies from their rear.

The Soviets Union showed little interest in supporting a ceasefire when the tide was in the Arabs' favour. Suddenly, while their satellites were transmitting the movements of the battling armies, the photographs revealed that the Israeli troops were encircling the Third Egyptian Army and about to encircle the Second Army. The Egyptian forces were facing a disastrous debacle and they were not even aware of it. Kosygin, the alarmed Russian president, flew personally to Cairo to disclose the dire facts to the Egyptian president, Sadat. Kosygin was now demanding an immediate ceasefire, using every possible threat, including military interference to stop the Israelis. The Americans were not interested in a conflict with the Russians, so they pressed the Israelis to allow food and provisions to the besieged Third Egyptian Army. On 22 October, the Security Council adopted Resolution 338, calling for:

"all parties of the present fighting to cease all firing and terminate all military activity immediately, no later than 12 hours after the moment of adoption of the Resolution, in the position they now occupy".

The Israeli army was occupying the West Bank of the Suez Canal at a distance of 60 miles from Cairo, and the Golan Heights at 15 miles from Damascus. The Egyptian Second and Third armies held positions on the East Bank of the Canal, but the Third Army was completely encircled by Israeli troops, under their mercy to allow them food and water. UN Resolution 338 also called for all parties concerned to start the implementation of the Security Council Resolution 242 immediately after the ceasefire, and also to start negotiations under appropriate auspices aimed at establishing a just and durable peace.

After long and tedious discussions, which included the mediation of Dr. Henry Kissinger, the American Secretary of State, a disengagement agreement was reached in 1974 between Israel and Egypt whereby Israel withdrew its forces from the West Bank of the Canal to 3 miles inside Sinai. At first Syria refused to negotiate, but finally accepted a disengagement agreement. Israel withdrew its forces from their position, 15 miles from Damascus, and evacuated the Syrian town of Quneitra, occupied by Israel since the Six-Day War. These agreements amounted only to a ceasefire, for no peace prospect was yet to be seen in the offing.

14

FROM THE SIX-DAY WAR TO THE OSLO AGREEMENT

A short time after the fire of the Six-Day War had died out Israel removed all barriers between Israeli and Arab areas in the West Bank. Moshe Dayan, Israel's Defence Minister, wanted to relax relations between the Israelis and their former foes. He ordered the army to take positions at the outskirts of Arab cities and that no soldier should be seen in Arab towns or villages. Israeli Arabs rushed to the West Bank and Gaza Strip to meet with old friends and family members after many years of separation. Tens of thousands of Israelis and Arabs toured each other's towns with great curiosity, and there seemed to be little sign of hostility between the two peoples. Israeli experts helped the Arabs to improve their efficiency and output by introducing modern methods to Palestinian agriculture and industry. Many thousands of Arabs came every day from the West Bank and Gaza to work in Israel, and their economy had never been better. But the Arabs states continued with their incitement against the Jews, and the Palestine Liberation Organisation

(PLO) with its many splinters soon renewed their terrorist activities against Israel.

In 1968, Palestinian terrorists hijacked an El-Al plane and directed it to Algeria. A month later they attacked another El-Al plane in Athens airport. In September 1970 they hijacked three passenger planes, of Swissair, TWA and BOAC, and blew them up in Jordan, which became the stronghold of the PLO. This atrocity was the last straw that broke King Hussein's back. He now ordered his army to throw the PLO out of Amman and the major Jordanian towns. After fierce battles and many casualties, Arafat was forced to flee with his remaining 2,000 men to Lebanon, where he established another stronghold, from which his terrorist activity against Israel continued with greater impetus. Among the hundreds of terrorist actions launched by his men, the most appalling were the brutal attack on an Israeli school bus at Avivim in May 1970, which left 9 children (aged 6 to 9) killed and 19 crippled for life; the massacre of scores of passengers at Tel-Aviv airport in 1972 by members of the Japanese Red Army who were acting on behalf of their Palestinian 'comrades'; the massacre of 12 Israeli athletes during the Olympic games in Munich in 1972; the massacre of 18 residents, including 9 children, in their homes in Kiriat Shmone in 1974; the massacre of 21 children at a school in Ma'alot in the same year; the massacre in 1978 of 35 innocent passengers of a bus on its way to Tel-Aviv, which was hijacked and set ablaze during the exchange of fire between the terrorists and Israeli soldiers.

In 1977, Sadat, the Egyptian president, surprised the whole world by visiting Israel. Following talks with Menahem Begin, the Israeli Prime Minister, the two leaders developed an amicable relationship. After difficult and lengthy negotiations,

Egypt signed a Peace Treaty with Israel in 1979, the first of its kind with an Arab country. Israel agreed to hand over all of the Sinai Peninsula to Egypt in return for the normalisation of relations. But most Arabs were not satisfied with Sadat's peace achievements and he became unpopular among his own people, as well as outside Egypt. Consequently, Egyptian fanatics showed their opposition in their usual way; three Islamic soldiers of the Egyptian army assassinated their president in 1981 during a military parade, in punishment for his accord with Israel.

As to Jordan, King Hussein had always believed that peace with Israel would bring his kingdom stability and prosperity. He had been involved in clandestine peace talks with the Israelis, but having lacked the stature of Sadat, Hussein feared the wrath of the Arab world if he signed a peace agreement with Israel while the Syrians and the Palestinians were still in a state of war with it. He therefore preferred to wait for the right opportunity, which finally arrived 15 years later, after the Palestinians had signed the Oslo Accord with Israel.

Meanwhile, the Palestinians in Lebanon intensified their attacks and started using Katyusha mortars against Jewish towns and settlements in Northern Israel, causing loss of life, panic and damage to property. In 1982, Israel invaded Lebanon after Palestinian terrorists shot and seriously wounded its Ambassador in London. Arafat, together with his organisation, was driven out to a new base in Tunisia. In this war, the Lebanese Christian Phalanges, who cooperated with the Israeli army in the fight against the Palestinian terrorists, committed a harrowing crime when they massacred in cold blood several hundred Palestinians in the refugee camps of Sabra and Shatilla. The Israeli army stopped the massacre when they became aware of it (the same day), but the army was nevertheless blamed for allowing the Phalanges to patrol the Palestinian camps in the first place. Consequently, the Israeli Government appointed a commission of inquiry, chaired by Yitzhak Kahan, president of Israel's Supreme Court, to investigate the events that led and caused the massacre. The Commission found Ariel Sharon, who was Defence Minister at the time, indirectly responsible, and as a result he was forced to resign his office. Israel's machine of justice was quick and decisive, and although the Israeli army had not been involved in the atrocity, the commission found Mr. Sharon indirectly responsible, not having foreseen the danger posed by the Christian Phalanges.

By contrast, in 1994, the Hutu majority in Rwanda committed genocide against the Tutsi minority. Major General Romeo Dallaire, the commander of the United Nations Peace Keeping Force in Rwanda, sent an urgent telegram, known as the "genocide fax", to Kofi Annan, but Mr. Annan did nothing to stop the murder. The whole international Community stood by, while the Hutus massacred one million Tutsis under their watchful eye. They had the men and the arms there, but they did not intervene to stop the massacre until one million men, women and children were slaughtered in cold blood. Worse still, and to the disgrace of the United Nations, no inquiry commission was appointed, nor was Kofi Annan forced to resign.

Between 1983 and 1985, Israel withdrew its forces from the captured area in Lebanon, except for a 'security zone', in order to block the Shia'ite Muslim group, Hezbullah, from staging attacks against Israeli communities in northern Israel.

In December 1987, the Palestinians started what is known as 'Intifada'. The literal meaning of the word is a 'shake-off', or 'uprising'. Palestinian youth in the occupied territories, incited by preachers in the mosques, started the insurrection. In the beginning it involved demonstrations, strikes, roadblocks and stoning, but no firearms were used. However, it did not take long before the PLO took command of the Intifada and turned it to an armed struggle, with the Palestinians using 'Molotov bottles', grenades, explosives and guns.[37] The Israelis tried to suppress the disturbances with police and army forces, but the protests continued for about 5 years and petered out only in 1992. In the course of this uprising, about 30 Israeli soldiers and civilians were killed in the Arab territories and many hundreds were injured. The main achievement of the Intifada, however, was to force the Israeli government to find a solution for the Palestinian problem. Israel, therefore, started peace talks with the Palestinian leaders in the occupied areas, but soon found out that they were subservient to the PLO in Tunisia and were not able to take any independent decision. Consequently, it was decided by the Israelis to start secret talks directly with the exiled representatives of the PLO.

The main intermediary of these talks was Terje Rod Larsen, the leader of the Norwegian Research Organisation FAFO, who had good connections with Palestinian leaders. Larsen conveyed the idea of Israeli-Palestinian talks to politicians of the Norwegian Labour Party, who in turn invited representatives of the PLO and the Israeli Government to an informal and relaxed meeting in a quiet suburb of Oslo, away from media attention. After lengthy negotiations, an agreement was reached and signed in Washington by Yitshak Rabin, Israel's Prime Minister, and Yasser Arafat, Chairman of the PLO, on 13 September 1993. The highlight of the Oslo Agreement was a Palestinian autonomy in the Gaza Strip and the West Bank, with an ultimate independence in those areas as a distant goal. Among others, the Oslo agreement stated:

"Both sides shall take all measures necessary in order to prevent acts of terrorism, crime and hostilities against each other…and shall take legal measures against offenders. In addition, the Palestinian side shall take all measures necessary to prevent such hostile acts directed against the settlements, the infrastructure serving them and the Military Installation area, and the Israeli side shall take all measures necessary to prevent such hostile acts emanating from Settlements and directed against Palestinians".

The Agreement clearly signalled the end of hostilities and armed struggle. It stated that disputes should be settled through the Liaison Committee, or otherwise, could be settled by a mechanism of conciliation to be agreed between the parties. And, if they cannot be settled through conciliation, the parties may agree to submit them to arbitration. It also stated that:

"The Council shall establish a strong police force…." and *"except for the Palestinian Police and the Israeli military forces, no other armed forces shall be established or operate in the West Bank and the Gaza Strip. Except for the arms, ammunition and equipment of the Palestinian Police described in Annex I and those of the Israeli military force, no organisation, group or individual in the West Bank and Gaza Strip shall manufacture, sell, acquire, possess, import or otherwise introduce into the West Bank or Gaza Strip any firearms ammunition, weapons, explosives, gunpowder or any related equipment, unless otherwise provided for by Annex I".*

In a signed letter dated 4 May 1994 to the Israeli Prime Minister, Yitzhak Rabin, Arafat promised that when he entered the Gaza Strip and Jericho Area, he would use the title 'Chairman of the Palestinian Authority', and not 'President of Palestine'. Arafat also undertook to submit to the next meeting of the Palestinian National Council for formal approval the necessary changes with regard to the Palestinian Covenant with the explicit purpose of abrogating the clauses that deny Israel's right to exist.

By the Oslo Agreement, Arafat clearly undertook to abandon terrorism and arrest terrorists, dismantle the terrorist infrastructure, collect illegal arms and end incitement against Israel. The Palestinian Authority was committed to solve the Israel-Palestinian dispute by peaceful means and negotiations. This was also made clear by a personal letter from Arafat dated 9 September 1993 to the Prime Minister of Israel, in which he wrote:

"Yitzhak Rabin,
Prime Minister of Israel

Mr. Prime Minister,

The signing of the Declarations of Principles marks a new era in the history of the Middle East. In firm conviction thereof, I would like to confirm the following PLO commitments:

The PLO recognizes the right of the State of Israel to exist in peace and security.

The PLO accepts United Nations Security Council Resolutions 242 and 338.

The PLO commits itself to the Middle East peace process, and to a peaceful resolution of the conflict between the two sides and declares that all outstanding issues relating to permanent status will be resolved through negotiations.

...the PLO affirms that those articles of the Palestinian Covenant which deny Israel's right to exist, and the provisions of the Covenant which are inconsistent with the commitments of this letter are now inoperative and no longer valid. Consequently, the PLO undertakes to submit to the Palestinian National Council for formal approval the necessary changes in regard to the Palestinian Covenant.

Sincerely,

Yasser Arafat
Chairman
The Palestine Liberation Organisation "

As the reader will soon see, this letter was a great sham. Arafat did not sign it, nor did he sign the Oslo Agreement, in good faith, but just to enable *'the Palestinian liberation Forces to fight the enemy from within',* as explained to the Palestinian students later in their text books.

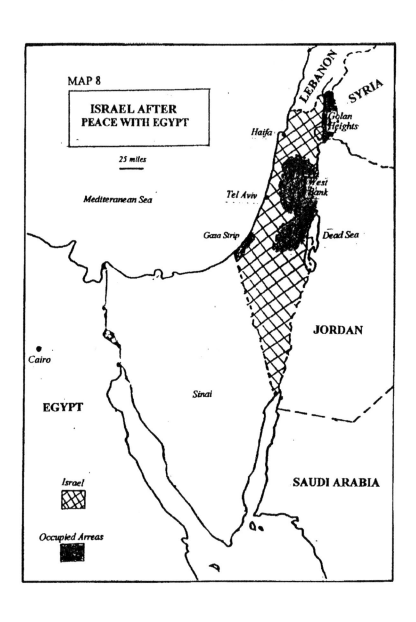

MAP 8

ISRAEL AFTER PEACE WITH EGYPT

25 miles

Mediteranean Sea

LEBANON

SYRIA

Haifa

Golan Heights

Tel Aviv

West Bank

Gaza Strip

Dead Sea

JORDAN

Cairo

Sinai

EGYPT

SAUDI ARABIA

Israel

Occupied Arreas

15

THE COLLAPSE OF THE OSLO AGREEMENT

Since Arafat arrived in the occupied areas, the Palestinians, under the leadership of their Chairman Arafat, have been persistently breaching the clauses of the Oslo Agreement. Following is a brief summary of their failure to honour their commitments:

1. The Palestinians failed to prevent the formation of armed forces other than "the Palestinian Police". Numerous terrorist organisations operated and are still operating in the occupied areas.

2. They failed to prevent acts of terrorism.

3. They failed to take measures against offenders. They deceitfully arrested perpetrators through what became known as a 'revolving door'.

4. They failed to prevent hostile acts against the Settlements and the infrastructure serving them.

5. Contrary to the Agreement, which limited the Palestinian force to a certain specified number of light personal weapons, they smuggled and secretly manufactured bombs, mortars, explosives, and a profusion of firearms. They even tried to smuggle anti-tank and anti-aircraft missiles with the ship 'Karina A'.

6. Instead of preventing hatred and incitement, they intensified both.

7. Contrary to the Agreement, they opened a Consulate in Jerusalem.

8. Contrary to his commitment in a signed letter to Rabin, 'Chairman Arafat' adopted the title of 'President Arafat'.

Despite the above breaches and continued acts of terrorism that worried the Israeli Government and Public, Israel still handed out the control of certain occupied areas to the Palestinians in line with the Oslo Accord, so that most of the Palestinian population became under the Palestinian Authority (PA) rule. Even when the right wing Benyamin Netanyahu became Prime Minister in May 1996, he transferred control of more areas to the Palestinians, despite his distrust in Arafat and the Palestinian Authority. Netanyahu, leader of the Likud party, was elected prime minister with a clear mandate to achieve peace with the Arabs. Having made little progress in this task, he lost the elections of 1999 to the leftist Ehud Barak of the Labour party, who vowed to withdraw the Israeli army from the 'Security Zone' in Lebanon, and make peace with Syria and the Palestinians. The choice of Barak reflected the aspiration of the Israeli electorate for peace with security. Barak was seemingly the most suitable candidate to achieve that. On the one hand, he had the credentials of an ex chief-of-staff and the most decorated soldier of Israel, and on the other hand, he was a left-winger who promised to withdraw from Lebanon and achieve piece within a short time.

Ehud Barak may have been an inexperienced politician, but he had some good qualities: he was shrewd, a good thinker and an excellent analyst. He believed that the piecemeal transfer of control of occupied areas to the Palestinians might turn out to be a pitfall. He wanted to know the end target of the Palestinians and what kind of state they had in mind. Accordingly, he challenged the Palestinians to negotiations with the aim of reaching a final peace agreement, which would result in a Palestinian state. It was obvious that Arafat was not interested in such an exercise. All his strategy, including the Oslo Accord, was based on deceit and on his plan of piecemeal liquidation of Israel; and along comes an apparently inexperienced counterpart to call his bluff. Arafat was therefore reluctant to accept this challenge, but the American President Clinton was anxious to move the peace negotiations forward. He invited the Palestinians with a degree of pressure on them to come to Camp David for serious talks with the Israelis. Arafat knew that if he refused, the blame would be put squarely at his feet, and if he agreed, he might have to face the moment of truth. He chose to accept the invitation.

The talks started in July 2000 and lasted for about two weeks. Contrary to the Israelis who arrived in Camp David with a detailed plan, the Palestinians arrived without any plans or proposals. During the entire talks in Camp David, it was the Israelis who made concessions and compromises while the Palestinians were only at the receiving end. Barak, having been anxious to keep his vow of peace 'in a short time', made far-reaching concessions. Gradually he offered Arafat far more than most Israelis would have agreed to. He offered to handover, not only 96% of the occupied areas, but, additionally, up to 3% from Israel proper, all of East Jerusalem, the Arab and Christian quarters of the old city and full autonomy on the Temple Mount. The extent of Barak's readiness for peace astonished the

Americans, but the Palestinians were not impressed. They wanted full control of the Temple Mount (promising to allow the Jews access to the Wailing Wall) and they did not budge on the 'right of return' of the Palestinian refugees to what is now Israel, which meant, to the Israelis, the destruction of their Jewish state. The Palestinians have the highest recorded birth rate in today's world[36], as opposed to a barely above the replacement level among Jews. Consequently, Israel has deep concerns about its future identity as a Jewish state because of the rapid multiplication rate of its own Israeli Arabs; if, in addition, Palestinian refugees were allowed to settle inside its borders, Israel would almost instantly cease to exist and an Arab majority would dictate the fate of the state.

Professor Shlomo Ben-Ami, the Israeli Foreign Minister and head of the negotiations team at Camp David, is a known leftist politician. As the negotiations progressed, he gradually realized that the Palestinians' end goal was not a state next to Israel, but instead of it. In an interview with the journalist Ari Shavit, which was published in the Israeli news paper 'Haarets' after the failure of the negotiations, he said:

"The basic assumption of all of us, including Ehud [Barak], was that in 1993 a kind of Palestinian state was established that would deal with us in accordance with conventional international relations. It transpired that that was a mistaken assumption, a wrong conception, as far as the other side was concerned. It transpired that 'Oslo' for Arafat was nothing but a gigantic camouflage, behind which he conducted, and still conducts, political pressure and terror in various doses, in order to undo the very idea of two states for two nations....Never did the Palestinians come with any counter offer, they never did, and they never will.

Consequently, the Israeli side was always in a dilemma: Either we get up and quit, because the other side is not prepared to make any offer, or we make another concession, another squeeze. Finally, even the mildest among us arrived at a point when one said to oneself: 'wait a minute', our counter parts do not seem to have any limit. Another squeeze and another squeeze, but it never satisfied them, and did not seem to have an end".

Before the negotiations ended in failure, President Clinton decided to make one last effort. He drew up his own peace plan, whereby everything Jewish remains with Israel and everything Arab remains with the Palestinians. But Arafat rejected this offer offhand. Raviv Drukker, a journalist who interviewed many of those who participated in the negotiations, wrote a book about the Camp David talks. He described how the indignant Clinton went to speak to Arafat, after the latter rejected his proposal. In his book, 'Harakiri', Drukker recorded the argument between the two leaders, in which Clinton admonished Arafat for not doing any concessions while Barak offered far-reaching compromises.[16] Barak accepted Arab sovereignty on the Muslim and Christian quarters of the old city, but Arafat wanted the Armenian quarter as well. Barak offered the Palestinians full autonomy on the Haram [Temple Mount], but Arafat wanted full sovereignty. The argument was quite acrimonious. Clinton threatened the Palestinian leader that he would sever relations with him, stop all aid and ascribe the PLO as a terrorist organisation, but Arafat did not budge a whit, nor did he offer any counter-suggestions. He simply waited for more concessions, which was of course frustrating to both the Americans and the Israelis.

It was therefore obvious to the Americans that they had heard nothing from Arafat in those fifteen days in Camp David to show that he was willing to reach a peace treaty with Israel. They realized that the Palestinians were not serious in their quest for peace and were not conducting the negotiations in good faith. It finally became clear that by his hackneyed and repeated slogan "peace of the brave", Arafat had meant that his counterpart should be brave, but not he. He was clearly afraid that he would be assassinated if he signed a peace agreement with Israel, and unashamedly asked Clinton: *"Do you want to come to my funeral?"*.[16] On the other hand, Barak showed great courage. He made such extreme concessions and unprecedented compromises, that when they were disclosed most Israelis were stunned by their extent. It would soon transpire, however, that those far-reaching offers would cost Barak not only his premiership, but his political career as well.

Looking now in retrospection at the results of the Palestinians' refusal of the most generous offer they have ever received, and on their decision to use gunfire and violence in response, it becomes evident that they have only suffered great losses and accrued no gains as a result. The Israeli electorate wrote off Barak in 2001, and Sharon was elected in a landslide vote to replace him as prime minister. Yasser Arafat, the Palestinian leader, lost his international status and became a humiliated prisoner in his half-demolished compound. The Palestinians lost control, not only of most of the areas but also of most of the Palestinian population that were under their control prior to the Camp David Summit. Their economy and infrastructure have been totally ruined. The Palestinian leaders, with Arafat at their head, have brought about much suffering, agony and bereavement to their own people, while achieving absolutely nothing, and losing almost everything. One cannot but remember Aba Eban's famous saying: *"The Palestinians never miss a chance to miss a chance"*. If they were committed to peace with Israel, they could have established an independent Palestinian state in Camp David, but it became more and more evident that their mind was not on a Palestinian state that lives in peace with Israel, but another, much larger Palestinian state that swallows the Jewish state, and, at a later stage, perhaps swallows Jordan as well, where the Palestinians already constitute a majority of the population there. This seems to be the real reason for the failure of the Camp David peace talks. Arafat came to the peace talks reluctantly. He did not want to discuss a final settlement. He knew he could not just yet achieve his dream of a state "from the sea to the river" and wanted meanwhile to continue the conflict. He preferred to hold on to his long-term intention while gaining control of as many areas as possible, leaving meanwhile the matter of the final peace settlement vague and undefined. He believed that under the circumstances, regaining control of lands was in itself a piecemeal liquidation of Israel that would, in time, make his final blow easier, while a peace agreement could tie up his hands. Barak, on the other hand, wanted to discuss the end product; the kind of state the Palestinian had in mind, and by so doing he forced Arafat to expose his true intentions to the whole world.

16

THE AL-AQSA INTIFADA

Arafat left Camp David and arrived in Gaza on 26 July 2000. As predicted, he was applauded by the crowds and received as a hero. On 28 September, Ariel Sharon, the leader of the Likud, the opposition party, went to visit the Temple Mount, the holiest place for the Jews, and the third holiest to the Muslims. Sharon's visit was approved only after Israel's Internal Security Minister, Shlomo Ben-Ami, had co-ordinated it with the Palestinian Security Chief, Jibril Rajoub, and received his assurance that no problems would arise, but Rajoub added that the Palestinian police would not interfere if violence broke out. Consequently, a contingent of Israeli police accompanied Sharon. The visit at the precinct took place at a time when it was open to tourists anyway. Sharon spent about half an hour in the open area. He did not enter, neither the al-Aqsa mosque nor the Omer mosque. During the visit, there were slight disturbances by Palestinian youth shouting slogans and throwing stones. Later on that day, after the visit, the stone-throwing intensified, leaving 28 Israeli policemen wounded and no harm done to any Palestinian. On 29 September, the Voice of Palestine, the official Radio Station of the Palestinian Authority, called upon all Palestinians to come and fight for the al-Aqsa Mosque. Arafat closed the schools and sent buses loaded with students to the Temple Mount, in what could only be described as an organised Palestinian riot. In the following days, and especially after the Friday prayers, the incitement and violence escalated.

The Palestinians claimed that the violence was a result of Sharon's desecration of the holy 'Haram al-Sharif' [Temple Mount] as well as unprovoked attacks by Israeli police, which invaded holy places and "massacred" innocent Palestinians. That was untrue. In fact the disturbances and the Intifada that followed Sharon's visit were a strategic decision by the Palestinian Authority taken after the Camp David talks. The Palestinians believed that by violence they could advance their aims. They believed that the Jews could not endure heavy loss of life, and would withdraw as they did from Southern Lebanon. This was a grave miscalculation on their part, since Southern Lebanon and the West Bank are like chalk and cheese. Barak had promised to withdraw from Southern Lebanon before he was elected prime minister, and Israel never had any affinity or claims to a Lebanese territory. On the other hand, the West Bank is of crucial importance to the security of Israel and without true peace or Jewish control, it could turn out to be an area of the gravest danger. In addition, the West Bank (ancient Judea and Samaria), is the heartland of Israel's birthplace, for which the Israelis retain great emotion. This perhaps explains why when they consider withdrawal from these areas the Israelis always speak about "painful compromises".

The Palestinian claim that Sharon's visit to the 'Haram al-Sharif' had been the main cause of the Intifada was refuted in

April 2001 by the American-European Mitchell Committee Report, which investigated the cause of the September 2000 violence and rejected the Palestinian claim. Later, the Palestinians admitted in the Arabic media that the Intifada was planned beforehand. Three months after the Temple Mount visit, the Palestinian Minister of Communications, Imad al-Falouji, spoke at a symposium in Gaza, and confirmed that:

"The Palestinian Authority had begun preparations for the outbreak of the current Intifada from the moment that the Camp David had concluded, and this was in accordance with instructions given by Chairman Arafat himself". Falouji went on to state that *"Arafat launched the Intifada as a culminating stage to the immutable Palestinian stance in the negotiations and that it was not meant merely as a protest to the Israeli opposition leader Ariel Sharon's visit to the Temple Mount".[17]*

The Intifada has continued since September 2000, during which time the Palestinians have used every means and method to kill innocent Israelis, with unimaginable brutality and savagery. They used suicide bombers, car bombs in Israeli cities, shooting rampages of gunmen in the streets of Israel's cities and towns, drive-by shooting and roadside ambushes, etc. The terrorist actions were indiscriminate; they massacred bus passengers, guests in pizzerias, young revellers in discothèques, shoppers in supermarkets, innocent people strolling in the streets, farmers in their fields, students in their universities, children in their schools, babies in their prams and mothers reading stories to their children in bed, but in particular aiming their blows at youth and children.

The Palestinian suicide bombers were encouraged and exalted by Arafat and other Palestinian leaders as being 'Shaheeds', i.e. martyrs, who sacrifice their lives for the sanctification of Allah and Islam. Their religious mullahs and muftis had issued a creed praising the suicide bombing and killing of innocent Jews as the "highest degree of martyrdom". Certain Arab states encouraged the Palestinian terrorists and supported and trained them to carry out these atrocities. Families of 'Shaheeds' received large amounts of money from certain Arab leaders and Arab 'philanthropists', as well as donors disguised as 'charity organisations'. Unspeakable hatred and incitement are spewed daily from Palestinian and Arab media, not only against Israelis, but against all Jews wherever they are, and the Western World look on indifferently, with equanimity, while this new form of heinous terrorism, anti-Semitism and Nazi propaganda is rampant.

After the Mitchell Committee's report had rejected the Palestinian claim that Sharon's visit to al-Aqsa mosque was the cause of the violence, the Palestinians came up with another claim; this time the violence was a direct result of the occupation. They, however, ignored the fact that Barak offered to end the occupation and that they were the ones who had rejected his offer. Prior to 1967, the Palestinians were under ruthless Egyptian and Jordanian occupation for about 20 years, and yet they never fought against it, or asked to end it. When, in 1970, during what is known as black September, the Palestinians started terrorist actions inside Jordan, culminating with the blowing up of three foreign aeroplanes, the Jordanians killed more Palestinians in two weeks than the Israelis have done in decades. The 'occupation claim' seems to be an excuse for violence, for Palestinian terrorism was rife before Israel took control of the West Bank and Gaza Strip in 1967, and even before the establishment of the state of Israel in 1948. Recall the rampant violence and attacks on Jewish life and property during the Arab riots of 1920-21, 1929 and 1936-39, and the increased Palestinian terrorism during the UN Partition Resolution of November 1947. After Israel's Independence War, Arab terrorism expanded further and between 1951-1956 Palestinian terrorists, who infiltrated from Egypt, Jordan, Syria and Lebanon, killed about 950 Israelis, all of whom were innocent civilians. Palestinian terrorism continued unabated even during the peace negotiations. In 1996, when the left-wing Prime Minister Shimon Peres was engaged in serious talks with the Palestinians, and peace seemed almost within reach, suicide bombers and car bombs caused hundreds of Jewish casualties and brought down the peace negotiations. As a direct consequence of the terror, the moderate Peres lost the elections to the right-wing Likud leader, Benyamin Netanyahu. This scenario of a terrorism wave repeated itself every time peace appeared to be in the offing, making it clear to the Israelis that Palestinian terrorism is not aimed at the 'occupation', but at any peace treaty with Israel, and at its very existence.

It is quite clear that a lasting peace between Israel and the Palestinians cannot be achieved without compromise and flexibility on both sides. It was so understood by the Israelis when Arafat came up with his famous slogan "peace of the brave". During the Camp David summit in July 2000, the Israeli Prime Minister, Ehud Barak, was determined to do everything possible in order to reach a peace agreement. To achieve this goal, he made unprecedented concessions, but the Palestinians refused to compromise. They did not come up with any counter proposal and wanted all their demands to be completely fulfilled. When they found that that was not possible, they packed up and flew back home. The failure of the summit, as bluntly stated by the Americans, was clearly due to the Palestinian unwillingness to sign a peace agreement that would provide security to the state of Israel. President Clinton was aware of the Palestinians' attitude and placed the blame for the failure of the talks squarely at their feet. Even the European countries, which had been normally pro-Palestinian, were critical about Arafat's rejection of the generous offers made to him by Barak. Arafat found himself isolated by both the Americans and the Europeans. He initiated the violence as a strategic decision, which, among other political purposes was to regain world sympathy, as they were the weaker side, even when they intentionally kill innocent civilians.

In order to shrug off responsibility for the failure of the peace talks, the Palestinian Authority started belittling the far-reaching proposals made by the Israelis at Camp David, denying that they were offered 96% of the occupied areas, plus additional territory from Israel proper, and claiming that the Israelis wanted the West Bank to be divided into cantons. Those who were present and involved in the negotiations refuted the Palestinians' charges. The US Special Envoy Dennis Ross commented on these claims by simply saying: "completely untrue".

By resorting to terrorism, the Palestinians have not only broken their Oslo commitment to solve all disputes by peaceful negotiations, but they have ruined any little mutual trust that may have existed between the two sides. Instead of solving the dispute through talks and compromise as agreed in Oslo, they chose to take action with fire and blood. The violence and terrorism of the Palestinians appears to be a strategic policy, aimed at destabilising Israel, sabotaging its social and economic structure and demoralising its citizens by mass and indiscriminate killing, so that the Jewish state will finally crumble and cease to exist. Recently, the Hizbullah leader, Sheikh Nasralla, confirmed this. In an interview with an English reporter, he said: *"the suicide bombing is working. Israel is disintegrating and it will not be long before it will be defeated".*

Knowing the Jewish value for life and particular love for their children, the Palestinians purposely target youth and children in order to inflict as much pain as possible on the Israelis. Pnina Aizenman, an Israeli young mother, had been standing at a bus station in a neighbourhood of Jerusalem when a suicide bomber from the al-Aqsa Martyrs Brigade, linked to Yasser Arafat, approached her and blew himself up. Her mother and her 5 years old daughter, Gal, were killed in the blast, and she and her 3 years old son were seriously injured. Mrs Aizenman is still haunted by the thought that the bomber stood by Gal *"because she was so pretty"* and that he aimed to kill children and babies.[55] On about the 21st of January 2004 an Israeli Arab waiter of Maxim Restaurant in Haifa, in which a female suicide bomber blew herself up, was interviewed on CNN. He testified that the bomber first sat down at a table and ordered a meal. After having finished eating, she called him and asked for the bill. As he was going to get the invoice he could see her getting up and walking towards a table with many children, where she exploded herself.

The reason for the deliberate killing of youth and children by the Palestinians seems to stem from Israel's withdrawal from Southern Lebanon. When Israel was still holding the 'security zone' in Southern Lebanon, several mothers of soldiers who served there got together and formed an organisation, which was later known as the 'Four Mothers'. They demonstrated against the 'security zone' and applied pressure on the Government to withdraw from Lebanon. Eventually, Israel withdrew its forces from there. To the Palestinians, the lesson was that the Israelis could not sustain the killing of their children and therefore the more children they kill, the sooner Israel would yield to their terms.

Israel often finds itself on the defensive for its occupation of the Arab territories and sometimes it is even indirectly blamed for the suicide bombing. Cherie Blair, the British prime minister's wife, spoke on the BBC television, saying that the suicide bombers committed their atrocities "out of desperation". The Liberal Democrat Member of Parliament, Jenny Tongue, announced on the 22nd of January 2004 that if she had been a Palestinian, she would have considered being a suicide bomber. This opinion seems to stem from deep sympathy with the appalling conditions in the Palestinian camps, which is wrongly thought to have been caused by the occupation. But this opinion ignores three facts: first, Israel does not want to rule over the Palestinians and had offered them an independent state, which they rejected. Second, the appalling conditions in the refugee camps were caused by the Arab states, which instead of absorbing their 'brethren' as Israel did to its Jewish refugees, they purposely kept them locked in squalid camps, in order to immortalise their problem for political reasons, and third, the Palestinians, with complete disregard to their poverty and misery, continue to have the highest birth rate in the world[36], thus exacerbating their own habitable and welfare condition.

Even without this explanation, one wonders what justification one can find for the deliberate killing of Jewish children and babies. Ms Tonge and Mrs Blair opined that the suicide bombers were driven to carry out their terrible acts of murder by "destitution and desperation". This opinion does not seem to hold in respect of the two Muslim Britons who went to blow themselves up in Israel, and who had both been enjoying comfortable lives in Britain. Neither did the September 11 terrorists seem to have suffered 'destitution and desperation' for they were all living in comfort in European cities. Also, there are literally hundreds of millions of people around the world, in Africa, Asia and Latin America, who live in conditions of penury and hopelessness, without generous donation and aid from the UN Relief Agency as enjoyed by the Palestinians, and yet they do not blow themselves up, or kill innocent people indiscriminately. I think that the cause of suicide bombing is to be found in the PLO's strategic policy of terrorism, the glorification of "martyrdom", the influence of the Islamic fundamentalist teaching, the brainwashing of the young generation to sacrifice their lives for Allah and Islam and the promise of the heavenly bounties awaiting them. The cause is to be found in the fanatic religious preaching that the killing of innocent men, women and children, is the "highest degree of martyrdom". It also has roots in the fundamentalist abhorrence of the 'infidels', their liberalism, democracy and way of life and last but not least, in the rejection of Israel's right to exist as an independent Jewish state amid the Muslim World.

As a prominent Palestinian once said: "Israel is strangling us, but the problem is that they cannot let go". This sad statement has been proven over the years. As soon as the Israelis remove check points, or open the border for Palestinians to work inside Israel, a suicide bomber blows himself up, killing as many Israelis as possible. That was exactly what happened at the Erez crossing when Mrs Reem al-Reyashi pulled the trigger off her explosive belt. At that time about six thousand Palestinians were trying to pass into Israel to work and earn some money. The Israelis claim that if they were to withdraw their forces, the terrorist organisation would gain freedom to carry out terrorist acts that would cost many more innocent Israeli lives. This claim must be given some credit. Under the constant threat of terrorism, it is a catch 22 situation for Israel. If it stays in the territories, it is acting against its morality and world opinion, but if it withdraws, it would endanger its citizens' lives. Israel's choice seems therefore to be not between the 'good' and the 'bad', but between 'the bad' and 'the worse', in which it is forced to choose 'the bad'.

The Palestinians adamantly refuse to disarm the terrorist organisation, and with the lack of a solution to this affliction, Israel has started building a security fence along the West Bank in order to stop suicide bombers. The fence includes a concrete section of about 4% of its length, in order to protect civilians from Palestinian snipers. Where the fence had been erected, it proved to be quite helpful, because the terrorists could not cross the border into Israel in ten or fifteen minutes as they previously did, but had to take a much longer way round in order to cross in places where the fence had not yet been erected. This gives a much longer warning-time to the Israeli soldiers to locate and stop them, as has been done in several cases. The efficacy of the fence has already been proven in the Gaza Strip, which was encircled by a fence many years ago. Terrorists could never cross into Israel from that area, and were forced to come from the West Bank. In some places the fence has encroached into Palestinian land, causing certain suffering to some families, but this should be weighed against the lives of the terror victims.

International law scholar, Stephen Schwebel, has opined that a country like Israel, acting in self defence, *"may seize and occupy territory when necessary to protect itself…and may require, as a condition for its withdrawal, security measures designed to ensure its citizens are not menaced again from that territory"*.[35]

There has been a lot of criticism about the security fence. Some even called it the Berlin Wall, although there is no equivalence between the two, for the one was aimed at preventing citizens from getting-out to freedom, while the other is aimed at preventing suicide bombers from getting-in in order to murder. The Israeli security fence is not the first or the only one of its kind. In 1969 a reinforced, corrugated steel wall was erected in Belfast to keep Protestant rioters out of the Catholic area. When it was erected, the then army commander, Sir Ian Freeland said: *"this will be a very temporary affair. We will not have a Berlin Wall or anything like that in this city"*. But, the wall proved to be very effective and 35 years on, not only has it not been dismantled, but another thirty seven (37) walls at interface areas have been erected, successfully keeping out the petrol bombs, home-made grenades, bottles and stones, all weapons which are far less lethal than suicide bombers. Not only Ireland, but Saudi Arabia is presently erecting a security fence on its border with Yemen to stop al-Qaida terrorists infiltrating its territory, and yet, no one seems to criticise these fences.

The obligation of a state to protect its citizens comes before anything else. Countries which are much safer than Israel do everything in their power to secure their borders, and Israel, which has been the victim of thousands of terrorist attacks across its borders, has the right to do so. When there was no terror, there was no fence, and when terror stops, the fence will have to come down. The source of the bad and the ugly is not the fence, but the terror. However, in its fight against terrorism Israel has always endeavoured to minimize the suffering of innocent Palestinians and in line with this policy it has already started dismantling and relocating parts of the fence which caused particular inconvenience to Palestinian civilians.

17

LEADERS AND CHILDREN IN THE VIOLENCE

In their war of terror against Israel, the Palestinian Authority has made heartless use of their children by placing them in the front line, and organising buses for their transportation to flashpoints. This immoral and illegal tactic has dual benefit to the Palestinians. First, the children serve as a human shield, behind which armed gunmen can shoot at Israeli soldiers. Second, it serves for propaganda purposes, which the Palestinians skilfully exploit, especially if Palestinian children are wounded or killed in the course of the violent clashes. The children's minds are poisoned by hatred and prejudice. While Israeli children are taught of co-existence and peace, their Palestinian counterparts are raised to hate Jews, and told: *"drop your toys and take up arms"*. Their textbooks are full of anti-Semitic expressions and inflammatory incitement against Israel. In order to boost the hatred, the textbooks include verses from the Quran, where Jews are defamed as corrupt, treacherous and enemies of the Prophet Muhammad. Zionism is described as a danger to the Arab world and a germ within the Arab nations, which has to be destroyed. The education system glorifies martyrdom and encourages Jihad against the Israeli "oppressor", relating stories of children eager to sacrifice their lives for 'Palestine', which is described as the whole of the pre 1948 area. The name 'Israel' is eradicated from the maps and the name 'Palestine' inserted instead. There is no trace on the maps even of typical Jewish cities like Tel-Aviv, Nathanya, Holon, Bat-Yam, Carmiel, Sderot, and others. The year 1948, when the Arabs rejected the UN Partition Resolution and threatened to throw the Jews into the sea, is described as the year of *"the greatest crime"* which created a *"state of bandits"*.

Students are falsely told that Zionists tried to burn down the al-Aqsa mosque in 1969 in order to rebuild their Temple. Hence it is the Arab "sacred obligation" to liberate the mosque from the "Oppressors". Palestinian textbooks do not mention Israel as a state, and their maps show the settlements only. There is a clear purpose in describing the whole of Israel as 'Arab Palestine'. Places such as Jaffa and Acre, which are in Israel proper, are referred to as "our homeland Palestine". The education system encourages Jihad, which it calls "the superior value", as a religious duty, and that all those who die in Jihad will be Shaheeds. Young Palestinians learn Sura 47 of the Quran which says: *"As for those who are slain in the cause of Allah, He will not allow their works to perish...He will admit them to the Paradise He has made known to them"*.

The Oslo Agreement is explained in the textbooks as a move that enabled the entrance of the Palestinian liberation forces into the territories in order to fight the enemy from within. This undisguised admission shows the lack of good faith and the policy of deceit adopted by the Palestinian Authority during the

Oslo talks. Such attitude wrecks Israeli trust in any agreement with the Palestinians, and makes them wary of any future settlement. Before peace can be achieved, there is inexorable need of a different, responsible leadership, prepared to honour obligations, and willing to stop terrorism and recognise the right of Israel to exist as a Jewish state in security and peace.

In their cynical use of children, the Palestinians have turned their summer camps into military camps, teaching children to be "holy warriors" and training them in the use of weapons and explosives. Certain camps train suicide bombers as young as 7 and 8 and brainwash them with slogans of Jihad and martyrdom. The Palestinians have proudly allowed foreign journalists to visit these camps, and the young future suicide bombers were interviewed and shown on TV screens all over the world. This manipulation of children is not only abjectly immoral, but is also illegal, being a violation of the international convention for the protection of children during armed conflicts and wars.

In Arafat's campaign of deceit, he has been playing a dual role, with two faces and two voices. When he talked to his people, or to the Arab media, he advocated the escalation of military struggle against Israel and used slogans, such as: *"Millions of shaheeds are marching towards Jerusalem"*[18] and *"Jihad, Jihad, Jihad"*[19] and *"If only Allah, Master of the world, would let me be shaheed among other shaheeds on behalf of Jerusalem".*[20,] and *"The gate to al-Aqsa is made of Iron, nobody but the shaheed will enter through it, Allah Akbar".*[21] These messages, and others saturated with fanatic Islamic slogans, add fuel to the flames, and are a clear encouragement for the escalation of violence and acts of terrorism and suicide bombing. On the other hand, when Arafat addresses the

American, European or Israeli public, he 'becomes' moderate and a 'peace lover'. In an article aimed at the Israeli Public, he emphasised that the Palestinian goal was to establish a state in the areas occupied by Israel in 1967; he expressed his will to resume peace negotiations; he shows understanding to Israel's demographic concerns, and condemns terrorist attacks against civilians, while at the same time he encourages 'martyrdom' and approves and funds suicide actions against Israel, as documents seized by the Israelis have proven. Not only Arafat, but other Palestinian leaders as well, use such tactics so as to appear mild and reasonable in their opinions to the Western world, while speaking of their true policies and aims in their native language. Even Mr. Abdel-Aziz Rantisi, the fanatical Islamist leader of the fundamentalist Hamas group, whose organization's declared policy is to destroy the State of Israel, tries to sound less fanatical to Western ears. After two Palestinian suicide bombers had killed 23 Israelis and wounded over 100 in Tel Aviv, he appeared on the BBC television screen On 6 January 2003, saying: *"the struggle will continue until they leave"*. He did not say, nor did the journalist ask him: leave what? The occupied territories? Or the whole of Israel, as he preaches in his Arabic sermons.

The reader will recall that Barak had already offered the occupied territories to the Palestinians, but they rejected the offer. This two faced tactic normally succeeds, for most Westerners may not be aware of the Palestinian leaders' speeches of hatred and incitement in Arabic. In a speech on the Sahar television in March 2002, Imad al-Faluji, a prominent Palestinian politician, said: *"there are no civilians in Israel; all the Israelis are enrolled...it is the full right of our people to strike in any place"*. Another politician, at the celebration of the anniversary of Fatah, said in the presence of Arafat: *"there will be no peace nor security, stability or life for any one, until we shall achieve...an independent state, cleansed from the cancerous tumour, and from the settlements, and with the full return of the Palestinian refugees".*[22] The Europeans who support Arafat seem to be oblivious of these intentions and proclamations.

Palestinian Islamic scholars and preachers contribute largely towards aggressive action by praising martyrdom for the sanctification of Allah and calling for Jihad. Preacher Muhammad Mustafa Najim said: *"we yearn to see shaheeds in all places, in order to free our land and restore the dignity of our people".*[23] He vilified the Jews as enemies of the Prophet who tried to poison, stone and murder him, and he called for Jihad and advised the Jews: *"look forward for your graves".*[23] The rhetoric is carried out by every possible means: speeches, sermons, TV and Radio programs, plays, songs, newspapers, caricatures, etc. By this incessant message of hatred, the Palestinians succeed in arousing great numbers of youth to violence and suicide actions against Israel. As a result of this brainwashing, and the generous rewards promised in heaven to those who die for the sake of Allah and Islam, the number of youth willing to achieve the 'glorified status' of martyrdom has escalated. Young Palestinians were enticed with verses from the Quran about the pleasures of paradise and the *"bashful virgins whom neither man nor Jinni touched before.."* and the *"bowls and ewers and a cup of purest wine that will neither pain their heads nor take away their reason"* and *"dark eyed houris [the beautiful virgins] chaste as hidden pearls".* Young Muslims, who by tradition and religion abstain from any sexual contact, can hardly turn down such temptation. Even their parents seem to have been influenced by this rhetoric, to the extent that they appear to celebrate their children's death. Such exploitation of young lives for political reasons is abhorrent to the Western mind, but it does not bother Palestinian political leaders, or their religious preachers, to take advantage of children's naivety (excluding their own) and convince them to blow themselves up. One wonders how long it would take to purge the minds and hearts of young Palestinians of the hatred and prejudice they have absorbed, and when will the right Palestinian leader arise to do that, and how many lives would be lost until then.

The Palestinian Authority, which endeavours to appear to be a responsible political organisation, had created the Tanzim militia (organ of Arafat's PLO-Fatah) to carry out terrorist actions against Israelis in order to compete with the Hamas and Islamic Jihad. The Palestinian Authority had provided the Tanzim with weapons, and authorised it to fire on, and carry out suicide bombing attacks against, Israelis. Documents seized by the Israelis at the PLO Headquarters clearly proved that Arafat funded the Tanzim, as well as al-Aqsa Martyrs Brigade[24], both being terrorist groups which have carried out over 1700 acts of terrorism and suicide bombing against Israel. Contrary to the Oslo Accord, the Palestinian Authority has been smuggling arms into the occupied areas and illegally producing weapons and ammunition in clandestine workshops, located in crowded residential areas. A large smuggling attempt of a huge amount of weaponry was revealed to the world when the Israelis intercepted and captured the 'Karina A' ship. Arafat appeared on the Egyptian television and denied any involvement in the smuggling attempt. He said that no one could prove that the ship belonged to the Palestinian Authority, and that he had no relation with the Iranians *"on that subject"*. The truth was that the 'Karina A' was a smuggling operation organised and funded by the Palestinian Authority, and the weaponry did originate in Iran, who also openly arms the Hezbullah of Lebanon. The master and the crew of the ship were all Palestinians from the Palestinian Naval Police, and Fuad Shubaki, the head of the Palestinian Financial Administration, was the man who funded the operation. Since Arafat is the only person in the Palestinian Authority to approve any money expenditure, it is inconceivable that such an operation, involving such a large amount of money and serious political risks, would have been undertaken without the knowledge and full approval of Arafat.

A former Palestinian Interior Minister revealed Arafat's involvement in violence. In an interview to The Globe and Mail, Abdel Razak Yehiyeh, who resigned from Arafat's government in October 2002, said to the Globe that he was prevented from demilitarising the police forces and was overruled when he tried to remove several commanders who had participated in attacks on Israel. He added that while Arafat speaks of the Palestinian commitment to end military confrontation with Israel, he opposes it in practice. Mr. Yehiyeh shocked some Palestinians with his frank denunciation of suicide attacks on Israelis, which he described as both *"tactically and morally misguided, and contradicts our religious, moral and cultural beliefs"*. He was, in particular, critical of the leaders of the militant groups, who sent their youth to carry out acts of suicide bombing against innocent civilians, but his voice was lost in a wilderness of fanaticism and militancy.

In contrast to their preaching, most militant Palestinian leaders who incite juveniles to carry out suicide bombing and achieve 'martyrdom', seem to be less prepared to die themselves as 'shaheeds', or send their own children on suicide actions. For reasons better known to them, they are not enthusiastic to reap the 'rewards in heaven' with which they have enticed their young suicide bombers. Some of these leaders, when confronted, chose to surrender rather than die in battle and become 'holy warriors'. Marwan Barghouti and al-Masri were two of many such examples. Barghouti, the head of Tanzim, and his deputy, al-Masri, who sent many youth to carry out suicide bombing in Israel, causing the death of many scores of Israelis, raised their hands when they were surrounded by Israeli soldiers, and surrendered in humiliation. Not one shot was fired and no attempt was made to achieve 'martyrdom'. They preferred to stay alive. They were both in custody at the time of writing these lines, awaiting their sentence at an Israeli court for war crimes. On the 29th of December 2002, Majd al Masri, the head of the al-Aqsa Martyrs Brigades in Samaria, the organisation responsible for many suicide-bombing actions, was arrested without any resistance. He did not attempt to escape or do anything that might endanger his life, and the list is long of Palestinian leaders who fill Israel's prisons, after having surrendered without a shot being fired. Even Chairman Arafat, who lured others to jihad and martyrdom and who has said: *"if Allah will only let me be a shaheed",* has no doubt used this proclamation only to entice naïve youth and juveniles.

18

INCITEMENT BY THE ARAB COUNTRIES

The Arab countries, including those that have a peace agreement with Israel, have joined forces in an unprecedented war of incitement and hatred against Israel and the Jewish people. This campaign is imbued with unspeakable anti-Semitic slogans, against which Nazi propaganda would have paled in comparison. The hostility is not aimed at Israel alone, but at the Zionist movement and the Jewish people wherever they are. Anti-Semitism in the Egyptian media has been thriving not only since the last Intifada, but since Egypt signed a peace treaty with Israel over two decades ago. Israel is being compared to Nazi Germany. Traditional blood libels against the Jews are related in the media with derogatory expressions. The Holocaust is denied and presented as an Israeli invention to *"extort Germany and eat away its resources"* and that it was only a myth and *"historians throughout the world have refuted Israeli claims in this regard and have proven that it was a fabricated story"*. All these accusations can be found not only in independent newspapers, but also in state controlled dailies. In March 2002, an Egyptian Government daily, which is distributed not only in Egypt and the Arab world, but is also sold in the streets of London and other European capitals, published an article about the Jews: it said:

"They are accursed in heaven and on earth...they are a catastrophe for the human race...They are the virus of the generation...They are the plague of the generation and the bacterium of all times...Their history was and always will be stained with treachery, falseness and lying...They are a model of debasement and degradation...If only you had done it brother [addressing Hitler] so the world could sigh in relief without their evil and sin".

In another article the same newspaper thanked Hitler for what he had done *"to the vilest criminals on the surface of the earth"*. Not only the Egyptian press, but also their Radio and television spew programs of hatred and anti-Semitism. The Egyptian television showed a serial, which they have also sold to 20 Arab countries, called 'Horseman without a Horse'. The serial is a revival of the anti-Semitic forgery of 'The Protocols of the Elders of Zion'. This false anti-Semitic document, which was published in Russia during the reign of Czar Nicholas II in the early 20th century, when anti-Semitism and pogroms were at their height in that country, was intended to divert the public anger from the government's failures to the Jews. The forged document claimed that the 'Zionist Elders' put down a program for the enslavement of the world and the destruction of the Christian civilisation and Religion. Of course, the Egyptian television added to it from its own imagination in order to make the Jews look as ugly and vile as possible.

Syrian incitement, found in their textbooks, the press and electronic media, surpasses that of the Egyptians. An Islamic education textbook from 1999 teaches the students about:

"The treacherous nature of the Jews and the obligation to eradicate them from the root", and that *"the Jews have contrived to kill, plunder and exterminate the Muslims. They yearned to do so because the Messenger of Allah had mercy upon them, and they saw in this forgiveness a way to betray the Muslims".*

The historical facts, however, prove otherwise. Upon Muhammad's arrival in Medina (The Hijra—622 AD) the Jews constituted about 60% of the city's population. They were prosperous and made a good living from agriculture (palm trees), industry, and commerce. They refused to recognize Muhammad as a prophet and he repaid them by depredation, extortion, expulsions and extermination; by the time Muhammad was in complete control of Medina, the wealthy and prosperous Jewish tribes of that city had ceased to exist.[41]

Syrian books on National and Socialist education from the year 2000 state that *"Israel is planning to expand its territory at the expense of neighbouring Arab countries…into Sinai, Syrian and Lebanese territories, and intends to reach the Euphrates and the Nile".* The Syrian Press uses anti-Semitic expressions and calls for the annihilation of Israel, which it says is *"a catastrophe and a huge threat to human civilization".* The Syrian Ambassador in Iran, Mr Turki Muhammad Saqer, spoke to Iranian students saying: *"America must recognize the fact that the annihilation of Israel is a religious obligation".*

Iran, the ex Sadam's Iraq, the Gulf Emirates, and even 'moderate' Jordan and Lebanon, do not lag behind Cairo and

Syria in the venom they expel. They use the same propaganda methods and the same anti-Semitic slogans. Israel is depicted as a dagger in the heart of the Arab world, and that it should be eliminated and thrown out of the region, like the Crusaders who were thrown out in the 13th century by the valiant Muslim fighters. Lebanon in particular serves as an important source of vitriolic propaganda against Israel and the Jews. Hitler's "Mein Kampf" has been translated into Arabic and distributed throughout the Arab world. The preface of the book states that *"Adolf Hitler is not only the exclusive legacy of the German people...he is one who almost stopped the course of history...he is therefore history's legacy".* The press and electronic media encourage terrorism and praise Jihad and the culture of martyrdom. Their anti-Semitic expressions and derogatory slogans against Israel and the Jews are unspeakable.

The Arab public does not question the authenticity of this vitriolic vilification. They often seem to accept not what is true, but what is pleasant to their ears. They indulge in lies as those of the 'Protocol of the Elders of Zion' that was translated into Arabic and distributed throughout the Arab world. They clearly find solace in this mendacity, and do not bother to question its authenticity. It is seldom that an Arab voice of dissention is heard, or a false 'fact' is loudly questioned, and if it is, it passes by like a voice in the wilderness, for one who raises a counter opinion may well risk one's wellbeing, and it is therefore safer to keep quiet.

The question is not whether the learned Editor of the Egyptian daily really believes that the Jews are *"a virus...a catastrophe for the human race...the plague of the generation and the bacterium of all times"* or, as the Syrian radio broadcaster claims, *"a catastrophe and a huge threat to human civilization",* for, as intellectuals, they must certainly know that that is untrue. The question is why do they feed their people with such lies? After all, as intellectuals, they should know that the contribution of the Jewish people to civilization and society is remarkable. The Jews constitute only 0.2% of the world's population, but since the establishment of the Nobel Prize in 1901, they have produced at least 128 Nobel Prize winners in Literature, Chemistry, Economics, Medicine, Physics and World Peace. In addition, Jewish contribution to music, art, film industry, theatre, philosophy, psychology and other fields, is outstanding. Suffice it to mention just a few musicians, as Mendelssohn, Mahler, Schoenberg, Bernstein, Rubenstein, Menuhin, Jascha Hefetz, Perlman, Zukerman, Vengerov, or a few artists, as Modigliani, Soutine, Pissaro, Chagall, Gertler, Libermann, Bomberg, Kitaj, Lucian Freud, or philosophers as Maimonides, Barukh Spinoza, Isaiah Berlin, Martin Buber, Hana Arendt, Raymond Aron, and the list is very long indeed.

One wonders why the Arabs, and the Muslims in general, who constitute about 20% of the world's population, have contributed so little to the world's civilization since their early days of glory in the eighth century. The reason, I think, is a reflection of their society not being integrated to the modern world. The immense progress in Western democracies in the last one or two centuries is mainly attributed to the freedom enjoyed by their citizens; freedom of fear, freedom of thought, freedom of speech, and freedom to criticize, which are all necessary conditions for intellectual accomplishment. By contrast, most Arab, and Muslim countries in general, are under autocratic or dictatorial regimes in which people are deprived of these liberties and the rulers steer the public opinion by state controlled press and media, in order to divert criticism or anger from themselves. For example, Most Arab media cannot criticise their governments for any failures, instead they put the blame on the colonialism of the past, the Americans, the Europeans, or the Jews. This was the situation in many countries in Western Europe about a century ago, and in Eastern Europe about a decade ago, before the people took control of their own destiny and established a democratic system conceived in liberty. Jewish Nobel prize-winners were fortunate to have been an integral and active part of one, or another, free and modern cultures, which their Arab counterparts, unfortunately, did not enjoy.

19

OPERATION 'DEFENSIVE SHIELD' AND JENIN

Since September 2000, the Palestinians have intensified their terrorist attacks inside Israel, causing a large number of casualties. The Palestinians' aim was to drive the Israelis to a breaking-point through an escalation in suicide bombing, rampaging gunmen and road ambushes. Indeed they succeeded in instilling fear and panic and disturbing the normal daily life of the Israelis. Routine activities, such as going for shopping or to a restaurant, taking a bus to work or school, or even just strolling in a street, became a life hazard. This long series of acts of terror culminated in March 2002, in which 130 Israelis were killed, including many children. On 27 March, the Israelis suffered the most heinous terrorist attack. As people sat down in the dining room of the Park Hotel in the town of Netanya, celebrating the first evening of the holy feast of Passover, a Palestinian terrorist entered the place and blew himself up, killing 29 and seriously injuring over 100. This large number of casualties is proportionally horrific to a small state like Israel.

Percentage-wise, it is similar to the Americans having suffered 1,500 killed and 5,000 wounded, in just one terrorist act. Loss of life during the Intifada was very painful to Israel, and March 2002 was the bloodiest month on record, but the Park Hotel massacre was the trigger to operation 'Defensive Shield'. The Israeli government, like any other responsible government, was determined to defend itself and the life of its citizens.

The main purpose of the operation was to take the offensive and strike at the terrorist bases and infrastructure, shatter their logistics and inhibit their ability to produce weapons and explosives. Also, the operation was aimed at arresting leaders of the terror groups, bringing them to justice, and gathering intelligence from them. The terrorists however chose to establish their bases and bomb-making laboratories inside crowded residential areas. To accomplish its mission, the Israeli army had no choice but to purge the nests of terror that were hidden among the civilian population, while taking every possible measure to avoid innocent casualties, often at the risk of endangering the lives of Israeli soldiers. It was decided to use infantry for the operation, instead of heavy weaponry or aircraft, which could have given better protection to the soldiers, but put Palestinian civilian lives at risk. Soldiers of the Israeli Defence Force are trained and taught to maintain the "Purity of Arms" and to fight in accordance with a certain code outlined in its doctrine, which says: *"IDF soldiers will operate according to IDF values and orders, while adhering to the laws of the state and norms of human dignity…and the value and dignity of human life"*. For these principles, Israel has paid dearly, for about 30 soldiers were killed and 130 wounded in the operation, all of whom lost their lives in house-to-house fighting.

As a result of operation 'Defensive Shield', many terrorists were killed and many others were arrested, including terrorist leaders who were on Israel's wanted list. Large amounts of weapons, ammunition, explosives, ready-for-use suicide belts, as well as bomb and weaponry factories were destroyed. After the three weeks of "Defensive Shield", Israel withdrew its forces under American pressure. It was clear that 'Defensive Shield' had not eradicated terrorism, since all the areas under the control of the Palestinian Authority have been turned into terrorist strongholds. Nevertheless, the operation brought about a period of calm in Palestinian violence, but it did not take long before the terrorists re-organized and resumed their terror campaign. Israel had once more to defend itself.

The refugee camp in the city of Jenin had become a notorious base of the terrorist organisations. About 25 suicide bombers came out of this camp and blew themselves up in Israeli populated centres. In addition, another large number of armed terrorists came from there to carry out indiscriminate shooting on Israeli civilians, and commit other acts of terrorism. Although the Jenin refugee camp was on the list of the Israeli army, it was last to be dealt with, which gave the terrorists ample time to prepare for the impending attack. They booby-trapped the houses, the streets, electrical posts, and even donkeys to be released towards Israeli soldiers and exploded at the right time. They placed snipers at strategic positions, and used civilians and children to shield themselves. The Israeli soldiers took every possible precaution to avoid harming innocent civilians. 55 Palestinians were killed in the operation, most of them fighters, while the Israeli casualties in Jenin alone amounted to 23 dead and many scores wounded. The Palestinian Authority, as in many other instances, succeeded in manipulating the Press. They announced that a massacre had been carried out, and that the Israelis killed 3,000 civilians in the fighting in Jenin. The Palestinian Authority issued misleading television pictures showing, falsely, that the whole refugee camp was destroyed, while in fact a very small section around the 'Casba' was damaged. The whole world was infuriated and Israel's denial was hardly heard, but gradually, and in the face of facts, the Palestinians reduced the number of dead to 500. It was only a few weeks later, after several investigations by the international media, that Mr. Kadura Mousa Kadura, a high-ranking aid to Arafat, was forced to admit that a total of only 55 Palestinians were killed in the course of the fighting.

Nevertheless, the Palestinians continued their claim about the 'massacre', and the UN Secretary General, Mr Kofi Annan, appointed a team to investigate the true facts about Jenin. Israel agreed to co-operate with the team, but demanded that the team should also investigate Palestinian terrorism, and Israel's right of defence. Following unsuccessful discussions, Mr. Anan called off the investigation. Meanwhile, respectable veteran journalists, the Human Rights Watch and the United Nations Organisation have investigated the issue independently and arrived at the conclusion that no massacre had taken place in Jenin.

The media has played a negative and irresponsible role in this episode. Most Western journalists have reported the Palestinian version. They passionately reported 'the massacre', not only without checking or verifying the allegation, but adding to it from their own emotion and superlatives. Their bias and animosity towards Israel was undisguised. Some examples of this reporting, which was reckless at best and dishonest at worst, is presented in the following chapter.

20

THE ROLE OF THE MEDIA IN THE CONFLICT

It is true to say that there has been biased reporting by the media, and particularly by journalists operating in Israel and the occupied territories, and the bias is clearly in favour of the Palestinians. The BBC, the Guardian, the Independent and the Daily Mirror in the UK, and CNN, Washington Post and Associated Press appear to take the Palestinian side in the conflict. These media agents, and several others, have adopted the Palestinian claim that the conflict is all about the occupation, and that Sharon's visit to al-Aqsa Mosque was the main cause of the Intifada. Sharon was never at al Aqsa Mosque, as he stood in the large open area of the Precinct, at a distance from the Mosque, and the Palestinians have admitted, anyhow, that they had prepared for the 'Intifida' for several months. I believe that the following are some of the reasons for this bias:

Firstly, some of the foreign reporters are of Arab origin, and as such their sympathy lies with their brethren. Suffice it to mention Fayad Abu Shamala, the BBC correspondent in Gaza, who openly said during a Hamas Rally: *"Journalists and Media organisations are waging the campaign shoulder-to-shoulder together with the Palestinian people".*

Secondly, some of the foreign reporters, who are not of Arab origin, usually suffer from ignorance about the region and do not speak Hebrew or Arabic. Such reporters rely on translators, or resort to reporting what they read in local English language publications, which may lead them to wrong reporting.

Thirdly, since Arafat arrived in the occupied territories, the Palestinian Authority tightened its hold on the foreign press. They made it clear to the foreign journalists that if they did not work with the Palestinian Authority (PA) representatives they would be denied any information and would not get interviews. Daniel Seamen, director of the official Israeli Government Press Office, said: *"At the direct instruction of the Palestinian Authority, the offices of the foreign networks in Jerusalem are compelled to hire Palestinian directors and producers. These people determine what is broadcast. The journalists will certainly deny that, but that is reality".*

Fourthly, foreign correspondents know that whatever they write against Israel, nothing untoward will occur to their wellbeing, but if they write against the Palestinians, they are risking their lives. Suffice it to mention that the Italian television photographer had to flee to his homeland, after he had published his film about the lynching of two Israeli reservists who lost their way in March 2000, showing their murderers bragging with blood on their hands. Another example is the double suicide bombing in Tel-Aviv in January 2003, after which the PA Security Forces arrested Al Jazeera's Gaza correspondent, Seif El Din Shahin, because he reported that Al Fatah was responsible for the atrocity. This was, of course, damaging to Arafat's credibility. The correspondent was released after 18 hours, and PA claimed that they arrested him only because he failed to reveal his source. Also, after the atrocity of September 11, the Palestinians took to the streets in Nablus, dancing and celebrating. The cameraman of the Associated Press Television News who filmed the event was threatened by Arafat's Cabinet Secretary, Ahmed Abdel Rahman, that if the footage was broadcast, the PA *"cannot guarantee his life"*. The cameraman begged his principals not to air the material, and Associated Press Television News caved in to the threats and refused to release the film. These are only a few examples, but it is a well-known fact that journalists in the West Bank cannot report something against the PA, without pain of punishment.

Fifthly, there is a natural tendency of certain reporters to side with the underdog, rather than report the simple and true facts.

And lastly, anti-Semitism and anti Israeli sentiment is endemic in Europe and England these days. This was confirmed by Mr Romano Prodi, the President of the European Commission, who, in February 2004, said: *"Anti-Semitic prejudice is alive and well. We can clearly see vestiges of historical anti-Semitism which was once diffuse throughout Europe"*. Sadly, some of those responsible for the media appear to be tainted by anti-Semitic prejudice.

Following are a few examples of the biased reporting:

1. The London Evening Standard during Operation Shield in Jenin: *"We are talking here of a massacre and a covering of genocide"*.

2. The Times of London on Operation Shield: "Rarely in more than a decade of war reporting from Bosnia, Sierra Leon,

Kosovo, have I seen deliberate destruction, such disrespect for human life".

3. The Guardian on Operation Shield: *"Israeli actions in Jenin were every bit repellent, as Osama Bin Laden's attacks on New York and Washington of September 11".*

4. Daily Telegraph on Operation Shield: *"Hundreds of victims were buried by bulldozer in a mass grave"*

Of course all this reporting was false, but even after it had been proven and widely acknowledged that there had been no massacre in Jenin, that the total number of the Palestinians killed was 55, and that the Israelis lost 23 soldiers in the fighting, not one newspaper had the decency to come up with an apology for the unspeakable false vilification of Israel. Following are a few more examples of media bias against Israel:

5. During the Palestinian rioting that followed Sharon's visit to al-Aqsa mosque, the Associated Press circulated a photograph of an angry Israeli soldier, with a baton in his hand, standing over a bloody young man. The caption, supplied by Associated Press, was: *"An Israeli policeman and a Palestinian on the Temple Mount"*, implying the cruelty of the Israelis and the suffering of the Palestinians. In fact the victim was not a Palestinian, but an American student, Tuvia Grossman, who was pulled out of a taxi, beaten and stabbed by Palestinians, and the photograph was taken after he had fled toward the Israeli soldier for protection; in addition, the photograph was not taken at the "Temple Mount", as the caption stated.

6. In Jan. 2002 two Palestinians rampaged through central Israel in a stolen car for three hours, with one driving and the other shooting randomly and killing innocent passers-by before he was shot dead. The Times of London headline was: *"Palestinian shot dead in Tel Aviv".*

7. The Hamas terrorist, Nasser Jarrar, who had earlier lost both legs and one arm while preparing a bomb to be used against Israeli civilians, was, in August 2002, targeted by the IDF and shot dead while preparing another bomb. The BBC's reporting of the incident was: *"Israelis kill an invalid Palestinian"*. ABC Radio referred to the terrorist as *"confined to a wheel chair"*, and the Washington Post headline was almost glorifying: *"..Legless, one-armed Palestinian dies shooting"*. No mention of how he lost his legs and arm and what he was doing when he got killed.

8. In March 2001, an IRA car-bombing took place in London, and in the same day a Palestinian suicide bomber blew himself up in Netanya. The BBC referred to the Irish terrorists as 'terrorists', but the Palestinian suicide bomber was referred to as 'militant'.

9. In October 2000, the 12 year old boy Muhammad al-Dura was killed in a fire exchange at the Netzarim Junction in the Gaza Strip while hiding with his father behind a barrel. The incident was widely reported in the Press and broadcast on the TV time after time, blaming the Israelis for the death of the boy. An investigation carried out later by the IDF, however, showed conclusively that the boy was not shot by Israeli soldiers, but by a Palestinian sharp-shooter and was filmed by a Palestinian television cameraman. By contrast, in March 2001, a Palestinian sniper deliberately shot dead in cold blood the 10 months old baby girl, Shalhevet Pass. The Associated Press' headline was: *"Jewish toddler dies in West Bank"*; as if she died of old age.

10. During the Jenin operation CNN reported that 30 pregnant Palestinian women died because Israeli soldiers held them up at check points. The source of this information was the

Palestinian spokesman Nabil Shaath, but CNN did not bother to check this fabrication. The true fact was that not one pregnant woman died at any checkpoint.

11. According to the Geneva conventions it is an offence for armed men to occupy a church, or any holy place to any religion, for purposes of war. When the Palestinians did exactly that in the Church of Nativity in Beth Lehem, there was not a word of criticism from the media, although the terrorists stole artefacts, desecrated the church and fired from there on Israeli soldiers. Hypocritically, all the criticism was aimed at the Israelis, who kept a watch at a distance.

12. A female BBC journalist reported on the twin suicide bombing in Tel-Aviv, in which 22 Israelis were killed. That was on BBC1 Television Channel on 6 January 2003. She concluded her report thus: *"Ya, But with the Palestinians it never stops. 50 of them are killed by the Israeli army every week".* This was a blatant distortion of the truth, for even by Palestinian count, the average during the Intifada was about 12 dead per week. Of course, even one dead is too many, but the BBC reporter had not only misled its viewers about the real number of casualties, she has also unjustly compared the targeting of terrorists by Israel, with the murder of innocent Israeli civilians by the terrorists.

Israel is under constant criticism and attack by the media despite it being a democratic country that operates under the rule of law, and is fighting for its survival against ruthless enemies. Of course, like in any other democratic country, mistakes are made and sometimes unlawful actions are taken, but basically, the government is obligated to abide by the rule of law and can be brought to trial if it does not. By contrast, there has never been a similar criticism against Arab countries or the

Palestinian Authority despite their autocratic regimes and systematic violations of human rights. In Israel, the courts have in many cases overruled the army and the government. For example, the Supreme Court overruled the army and prohibited the extraction of information from captured terrorists by physical pressure, even if this may be necessary to save innocent lives. As I write these lines, the Supreme Court, in response to a request from a civil rights group, overruled the Government and extended a freeze on building a 15-mile section of the security fence around Palestinian villages, north-west of Jerusalem. Also, Israel's Public Prosecutor has recently recommended prosecuting the Prime Minister Sharon for bribery and it is now in the hands of the General Attorney to either decide in favour of the state prosecutors, or find the legal evidence lacking. These are only a few examples demonstrating Israel's democracy, which are unthinkable in countries like Syria, Egypt, Jordan, Saudi Arabia, Morocco, Algeria, Tunisia, Bahrain, United Arab Emirates, Yemen and other Arab countries.

Unfortunately, the editors of the media possess the power to force their political opinion and inclinations on the Public. They sometimes do that at the cost of distorting facts, which is contrary to the ethics of their profession. Most people believe what they read in the newspapers, or hear on the radio, for it is the general assumption that journalists report the facts impartially, as indeed they are supposed to do. Sadly, this is not always the case. While the basic principle of reporting is to state the facts and leave it to the readers to form their opinion, some journalists nowadays seem to believe that it is their duty to lead a crusade for their own opinion, or their editor's opinion, or, in some cases, the opinion or interest of the proprietor of the paper.

21

THE LEGALITY OF TARGETING TERRORISTS

Since the beginning of the second 'Intifada', the Palestinians have been carrying out a brutal war of terrorism against Israel. The extensive use of suicide bombing in Israeli cities was aimed at causing the maximum loss of innocent life. They fill their explosive belts with steel bearing balls, nails, bolts and nuts, in order to maximize the number of Jewish casualties. They deliberately choose crowded places, aiming their strikes particularly at youth and children in school buses, discothèques, pizzerias and other entertainment centres. Their main purpose is to destabilize the State of Israel by causing pain, panic, demoralization and economic crisis. They carry out their attacks with complete scorn for international and moral laws. They establish their bases and their illegal weapon factories in crowded civilian areas and transport their terrorists and explosive belts hidden in ambulances. They shoot on Israelis from residential houses, churches and mosques. Forced to defend itself and the life of its citizens, Israel has been confronted with the moral challenge of fighting the terrorists, with minimum harm to innocent civilians. Hence, Israel resorted to pinpoint targeting by which it succeeded in eliminating a significant number of the most notorious leaders of the terrorist organisations; those with blood on their hands, and, more importantly, those who plan and encourage others to commit the atrocities.

It is audacious, but perhaps understandable, that the Palestinian terrorist organisations, which do not shy from killing indiscriminately by the most heinous methods, had the presumption to complain about the Israeli targeting of some of their most vicious members. It is, however, un-understandable and hypocritical, that countries, such as England and France, have joined them in criticising the targeting of terrorists by Israel, for, in less severe circumstances, France resorted to extensive torture in fighting the Algerian terrorists in the 1950s, and Great Britain, fought terrorism in Palestine with an iron fist, hanging people, bombing villages and destroying over two thousand houses of terrorists, and of those who aided them.[58]

Is the targeting of terrorists who have carried out, or were planning to carry out, or who had sent others to carry out murderous acts against civilians, a legal self-defence action? This is a question of International Law, which is beyond the capability of the author of this book, but the question had been dealt with by three celebrated American experts, who have looked into this issue and came up with the loud and clear conclusion that *"Suicide attacks are war crimes, targeted killings are not".*[25] Their full comprehensive report was published in the 'Jerusalem Post'; among others, it says that the Law makes a clear distinction between civilian victims deliberately targeted, and civilians killed in the course of attacks against legitimate military targets. Also, the killing of terrorists, militants, belligerents or military leaders, is legitimate at any time, on or off the battlefield. The fighting between the Palestinians and the Israelis has been categorized in the report as a 'war' and *"that being the case, both Israel and the Palestinians are bound by the laws of war in their operations, and the legality of their actions must be judged by that standard"*.[25] Suicide attacks against civilians are obviously not only a war crime, but particularly a crime against humanity. The fact that attacks on civilians may be the only means by which one side can effectively prosecute a war, does not make them lawful, especially as Israel had indicated its willingness to accept the creation of an independent Palestinian state. On the other hand, Palestinian casualties occurring during military operations do not violate the laws of war, so long as those operations have been carried out in accordance with the principles of distinction and proportionality. The experts determined that Israel's attack on Salah Shehadeh, for example, which resulted in a number of civilian casualties, was legally justified because Shehadeh was a highly important Hamas commander, responsible for numerous attacks on Israeli civilian targets. Finally, the report concludes by saying that the deliberate attacks on Israeli civilians, whether involving suicide elements or not, constitute a profound violation of international law. The individuals engaged in such attacks, and their political and military commanders, are war criminals.

This conclusion, by International Law experts, is certainly of great weight and importance, but one does not have to be a law expert in order to reach a similar conclusion, for it is only logical that the law would not bind the hands of people who are attacked and murdered indiscriminately and prevent them from defending themselves, only because the murderers who plan and commit the crimes act from, or hide in, civilian areas. If this was the case, then a band of terrorists could annihilate a whole population, feeling completely immune against any punishment by just seeking refuge among their supportive civilian comrades. Therefore, it is quite logical that the law should allow the offended party to defend itself even if some civilian casualties occur during the operation, providing that such operation does not violate the laws of war, and is carried out in accordance with *"the principles of distinction and proportionality"*.[25]

Another legal expert, Alan Dershowitz, a celebrated Professor of Law at Harvard Law School, has also responded to the question of whether targeted assassination of terrorist leaders is lawful; he stated: *"Targeting the military leaders of an enemy during hostilities is perfectly proper under the laws of war, which is what Israel—as well as the United States and other democracies—has done"*.[59]

I find the so called 'spiritual', or 'political', leaders of terrorist organisations, such as Osama Bin Laden, Mullah Muhammad Omer, Zawahiri, Ahmed Yassin, Abdel-Aziz Rantisi and their like, more dangerous and far more guilty of human crimes than any of their military commanders, or suicide bomber. They perhaps do not wear the explosive belts themselves, but they are the ideologists of terror; they preach, justify and encourage the killing of innocent people, and with their charisma and influence they succeed in convincing others to commit the crimes. Such Muslim 'spiritual' leaders have been operating not only in the West Bank and the Gaza Strip, but also in Europe, England and the United States. For example, in addressing a Muslim public in 1990, Sheikh Fayiz Azzam from Atlanta said to his audience: *"Allah's religion—be he praised—must offer skulls, must offer martyrs. Blood must flow. There must be widows, there must be orphans. Hands and limbs must be cut...* ". Such words, which were aimed at urging the audience to take action for the sake of *"Allah's religion"*, may have instigated the Islamic terrorist cells in America, which started with the blowing up of a van filled with half a ton of high explosives in the basement of the World Trade Centre in 1993, and culminated with the atrocity of September 11.

22

THE MAIN OBSTACLES FOR PEACE

Israel is often accused of intransigence. It is claimed that if Israel would only dismantle the settlements, withdraw its forces from the occupied areas and accept a Palestinian state in the West Bank and the Gaza Strip, that would be the end of the conflict, and peace would prevail. This claim ignores some historical facts, as well as the Palestinians' rejection of Barak's offer in Camp David. The real main obstacle for peace is not the occupation or the settlements, but the Arab's rejection of Israel's right to exist. Throughout the last century the Arabs have persistently rejected cooperation and peace offers made to them by Jewish and Israeli leaders. Tragically, they often woke up a bit too late to regret their previous refusals. Here is a short resume of the Arab intransigence:

1. As early as 1919, the General Syrian Congress sent a memorandum to the King-Crane Commission, which was appointed by the American President Woodward Wilson regarding the mandate in Palestine. They wrote: *"We oppose the pretensions of the Zionists to create a Jewish state in the southern part of Syria, known as Palestine, and oppose Zionist migration to*

*any part of the country…we consider them [the Zionists] a grave
peril to our people from the national, economical, and political
points of view".⁵²*

By contrast, the Zionist aims, as confirmed in a resolution at
their congress in Carlsbad, emphasized: *"the determination of the
Jewish people to live with the Arab people on terms of mutual
respect, and together with them to make the common home into a
flourishing community, the up-building of which may assure to
each of its peoples an undisturbed national development".*

One single Arab voice could be heard, however, which
sounded contrary to the 'Syrian Memorandum'. Emir Faisal,
who was proposed by the Syrian Congress to be the future king
of 'Great Syria', had signed an agreement with the leader of the
Zionist movement, Dr Chaim Weizmann, on 3 January 1919
(6 months before the Syrian Memorandum), in which he agreed
that: *"..all such measures shall be adopted as will afford the fullest
guarantees for carrying into effect the British Government
Declaration of 2 November 1917 [the Balfour declaration]. All
such measures shall be taken to encourage and stimulate
immigration of Jews in Palestine on a large scale, and as quickly as
possible to settle Jewish immigrants upon the land through closer
settlement and intensive cultivation of the soil".*

It is true that Faisal had signed this agreement, which was in
complete accord with the Balfour Declaration, but at the time
he was only an Emir, without a territory, trying to please the
British in order to be made king of 'Greater Syria'.
Nevertheless, Dr. Weizmann was enthusiastic about the
agreement and thought it was a great achievement, although it
was clear to the Jews of Palestine that the Emir could not be
relied upon, and that the *"agreement was not worth the paper on
which it was written".* As it happened, the Syrian dream of

'Great Syria' did not materialize. Faisal was made king of Iraq in 1921 and later denied having written *"anything of that kind with his knowledge"*.[52]

2. In April 1934, Ben-Gurion, head of the Jewish agency in Palestine, met with the 'moderate', influential Palestinian leader Musa Alami. Ben-Guriun offered the Arabs a hand of peace and co-operation. He suggested that such co-operation between the two peoples would bring about great agricultural, economical and technological development to the Arabs of Palestine (They were not known as Palestinians at that time, and not until 1967). Musa Alami's reply was blunt and clear: *"We prefer to remain poor and our land arid for another 100 years, until we, the Arabs, can achieve technological development by ourselves, rather than achieve it now with you"*. Ironically, Musa Alami, as well as the ultra nationalist and fanatic al-Husseini's family, had sold Arab lands they owned to the Jews in Palestine.[58]

3. In 1936, amid the Arab riots in Palestine, the British Government appointed Lord Robert Peel as head of a commission to find a solution to the Jewish-Arab problem. In 1937 the Peel Commission recommended the partition of Palestine into an Arab state, a minute Jewish state, and a neutral "sacred-site" around Jerusalem, to be administered by Britain. The Jews reluctantly accepted Peel's recommendation, but the Arabs rejected it offhand. During his questioning by the Commission, Ben-Gurion emphasized the peaceful aims of the Zionists and suggested that a *"Jewish free nation in Palestine would bring about great benefit to the Arabs"*. By contrast, the Arab representative vowed to do everything possible to quash Zionism.

4. When the Partition Resolution was presented for voting at the United Nations' General Assembly in November 1947, The

Palestinians rejected it, although it allotted only a small and vulnerable portion of land to the Jews. The Arabs proclaimed: *"any line of partition would be a line of fire and blood".*[10]

5. After Israel's victory in the War of 1948, the Jordanian king, Abdullah, was about to sign a peace treaty with Israel, whereby Israel would grant Jordan free access to its ships at the Israeli port of Haifa. The Palestinians, who, as usual, opposed any tolerance or peaceful attitude towards Israel, murdered King Abdullah while he was saying his Friday prayers in al-Aqsa mosque in East Jerusalem.

6. After the Six-Day War, Israel offered a hand of peace to the Arabs. They responded with the well-known 'three NOs Resolution' taken by the Arab League in Khartoum: *"No Negotiations; No Recognition and No Peace with Israel".*

7. After the Six-Day War, Israel offered the Palestinians agricultural and technological help. There was a short period of response in the late sixties and early seventies, from which the Palestinians benefited tremendously, but things changed when the PLO strengthened its grip on the occupied territories.

8. In July 2000, the Israeli Prime Minister, Barak, offered the Palestinians almost all their apparent wishes, i.e., 96% of the West Bank (plus compensation with other land from Israel), the Gaza Strip (with access to the West Bank), East Jerusalem, the Arab and Christian quarters of the old city and full autonomy on Haram al-Sharif [The Temple mount]. Arafat rejected the offer and started the Intifada.

One of the obstacles for peace is mistrust. The Palestinians have done very little to establish such trust. On the contrary, they have done everything possible to breed hatred and prejudice against Israel. They breached almost every agreement they had signed, and in particular their commitment to abandon terrorism and incitement against Israel.

The Palestinian Authority proved to be unreliable and corrupt. Billions of dollars which had been donated to them in order to revive their economy and fight poverty and alleviate the refugees' suffering, ended up in their leaders' pockets, on illegal acquisition of weapons and on funding terrorism. To assuage their people's anger, they have used lies as a political strategy to demonise Israel, which according to the Palestinian propaganda is the sole culprit for all Palestinian ailments and misery; consequently, its annihilation is the only way to Palestinians' relief and prosperity. They have bred a generation of suicide bombers and 'jihad martyrs' with the aim of terrorising the Jewish population and destabilizing their state, so that they can eventually destroy it and build a Muslim one on its ruins. They have addressed the Western World with deceitful conciliatory expressions of moderation, pretending to only want a "State next to Israel", while preaching the opposite to their own people and younger generation. Listening to what Palestinian leaders relentlessly preach in their native language, one would understand Israel's reluctance to take any risk with such a peace 'partner', who deceitfully aims at destroying it. Here are a few self-explanatory statements of some senior Palestinian officials, which they made to their people and Arab audience, clearly revealing their real intentions:

1. Abd el-Aziz Shahian, Palestinian Authority Minister of Supplies: *"The Palestinian people accepted the Oslo agreements as a first step and not as a permanent settlement, based on the premise that the war and struggle in the land is more efficient than a struggle from distant land* [Tunisia, where they were given refuge after the Lebanon war]...*the Palestinian people will continue the* *struggle until they achieve the goals of the 65 revolution"*—Al Ayyam, 30 May 2000. [The 1965 revolution is the founding of the PLO and the Palestinian charter for the destruction of Israel by armed struggle].

2. Sheikh Ikrima Sabri, Palestinian Authority appointed Mufti of Jerusalem and Palestine: *"We are discussing the current problems and when we speak about Jerusalem it does not mean that we have forgotten about Hebron, or Jaffa, or Acre…we are speaking about the current problems that have priority at a certain time. It does not mean that we have given up…We have announced a number of times that from a religious point of view Palestine, from the sea to the river, is Islamic"*. (Speech on 11 January 2001).

3. Faisal Husseini, Palestinian Authority Representative for Jerusalem affairs (meanwhile deceased): *"This effort [the intifada] could have been much better, broader, and more significant had we made it clearer to ourselves that the Oslo agreement, or any other agreement, is just a temporary procedure, just a step towards something bigger…We distinguish the strategic, long term goals from the political phased goals, which we are compelled to temporarily accept due to international pressure…Palestine according to the higher strategy is from the river to the sea. Palestine in its entirety is an Arab land, the land of the Arab nation"*. (al-Arabi—Egypt, 24 June 2001).

4. Abdullah al-Hourani, Chairman, Palestinian National Council Political Committee. Asked by the interviewer of al-Hayat al Jadida, on 14 April 2001, as to how he read the future of the peace process, he answered: *"Whether they return to negotiations or not, and whether they fulfil the agreements or not, the political plan is a temporary agreement, and the conflict remains eternal, will not be locked, and the agreements being talked* *about are regarding the current balance of power. As to the struggle, it will continue. It may pause at times, but in the final analysis, Palestine is ours from the sea to the river".*

5. Salim Alo'aida Abu-Salam, Supervisor of Political Affairs: *"When we picked up the gun in 65 and the modern Palestinian Revolution began, it had a goal. This goal has not changed and it is the liberation of Palestine".* (al-Hayat al-Jadida, 14 April 2000).

6. Othman Abu Arbiah, Director General for National affairs and Yasir Arafat's Deputy: *"At this stage we will prevail in our struggle toward the goals of the stages [plan]. The goal of this stage is the establishment of the independent Palestinian State, with its capital in Jerusalem. When we achieve this, it will be a positive step and it will advance us to the next stage via other ways and means...Every Palestinian must know clearly and unequivocally that the independent Palestinian state is not the end of the road. The rise of the Palestinian state is a stage after which there will be another stage and that is the democratic state in all of Palestine".* (al-Hayat al-Jadida, 25 November 1999—al-Hayat al-Jadida is a Palestinian daily.).

Together with their final goal of destroying the Jewish state, the Palestinians have also been running a deliberate vilification campaign against Israel, using false information and canards in order to demonize the Jewish state in the eyes of their own people and the whole World. Such policy increases the mistrust and enmity and cannot be conducive to peace. Here are a few examples of such malicious denigration:

1. Hundreds of emails have been sent to European and British addresses claiming that Israeli soldiers had raped a pregnant woman, along with another 86 non-pregnant women. This utterly false allegation was also posted on the website of a

British MP, who used it to illustrate the "moral bankruptcy" of Israel's actions.

2. The infamous, false 'massacre' allegation, spread during the Jenin operation by Arafat's chief aide, Saeb Arakat. In the same breath of shouting 'massacre', the Palestinians claimed that the battle was a great victory and Arafat proudly called it "Jeningrad", after the heroic Russian battle against the Nazis in Stalingrad.

3. Blood libels, as if the 'Talmud' states that *"the matzos of Passover must be kneaded with blood from non-Jews. The preference is for the blood of youth after raping them".* Naive people may take such nonsense at face value.

4. Claims that Israel has been bringing Russian Jewish girls infected with Aids into Palestinian territories in order to infect their innocent Palestinian men.

5. Claims that Israel distributed to the Palestinians food laced with viruses and poisons ('Al Hayat al Jadida' 22.8.1998) and that Israel used "black gas" and depleted uranium against them (Suha Arafat 11.11.1999). Such lies were trumpeted in the media, but when refuted by Israel, they received but little echo.

6. Accusations that Israeli soldiers broadcast pornographic material on al-Watan Telivision in Ramalla.

7. The Palestinians deny the Jewish history in the Holy Land. They deny the Jews' rights on Jerusalem (although the Jews have been a majority in Jerusalem) and the Land of Israel, despite the fact that the Jews have been the inhabitants of this land from time immemorial and have been living on it, as a majority or a minority, for 4,000 years. They deny that there was a Jewish kingdom for hundreds of years with Jerusalem as its capital. They also deny that there was a Jewish temple that stood on the Temple Mount, where Muslims later built their Aqsa Mosque. This, despite the fact that the long history of the Jewish people in Israel is recorded in the Bible, in some verses of the Quran, in Egyptian and Babylonian documents and in ancient history books (as those of Plavius Josephus, for example), and has been corroborated by extensive excavations and papyruses. By contrast, the Palestinian right to an independent state is questionable. There has never been a sovereign Arab entity called 'Palestine'. In late history, the land was under the rule of the Ottoman Empire for 400 years and then for another 30 years under the rule of Britain, whose mandate was to establish a Jewish state. Until about 1920, the Arabs in Palestine, including the nationalist Haj Amin al-Husseini, identified themselves with 'Greater Syria'. Prior to the Six-Day War, Jordan and Egypt controlled the West Bank and Gaza Strip respectively, annexing, or turning, these areas into parts of their territory, without any protest on the part of the Palestinians. As to the holy city of Jerusalem, the Quran does not mention 'Jerusalem' even once, while it is mentioned hundreds of times in the Old Testament, and has always been the heart and soul of the Jewish people for at least 15 centuries before the birth of Islam. Nevertheless, and contrary to the Palestinian uncompromising attitude, Israel recognizes the Palestinian right on this land and has already declared its acceptance of a peaceful Palestinian state next to it.

It is not only the spoken word in Arabic that worries Israel, but it is also the written tenets of the PLO that explicitly call for armed struggle as the "only means of liberating Palestine", which is claimed to be "an indivisible part of the Arab homeland". Al-Fatah also sets out its objective to wipe out the "existential trace of this artificial phenomenon", and, as expressed by a high-ranking officer in the command of the PLO, *"to re-occupy the usurped land regardless of the method be it to smashing or annihilation"*.[52] Similarly, the Hamas Charter explicitly rejects any compromise with Israel, which, it says is contrary to the Islamic law, and calls for a holy war as the only solution for liberating 'Palestine' that they claim is an Islamic 'wakf' [trust] on all Muslims until doomsday.

It is of interest that the Palestinians, and particularly the fundamentalists among them, use verses and passages from the Quran and the Hadith to disparage the Jews and justify fighting and killing them, but ignore other verses which state that 'Palestine' was given to the Jews by God.

Sura 5 of the Quran, for example, says: *"Bear in mind the words of Moses to his people. He said: Remember, my people, the favour that God has bestowed upon you. He has raised up prophets among you, made you kings and given you that which He has given to no other nation. Enter then, my people, the Holy Land that God has ordained for you, and do not turn back, or you will lose"*.[56]

Sura 17 of the Quran refers to the return of the Jews from exile (in this case from Egypt) to their Promised Land. Moses said to Pharaoh: *"Indeed Pharaoh, I can see that you are doomed. He sought to scare them out of the land, but We drowned him together with all who were with him. Then We said to the Israelites: Dwell in the land. When the promise of the hereafter comes to be fulfilled, we shall assemble you all together"*.[56]

In the Oslo Agreement, Arafat had undertaken to abolish such clauses in the PLO Charter that denied Israel's right to exist, or called to destroy the Jewish state, but, as in many other cases, he did not keep his promise. Instead, he has been poisoning the minds and hearts of young Palestinians with hatred. Arafat had not evoked much trust. He 'condemns' terror, but supports and funds it; he talks peace and at the same time preaches: 'jihad', 'jihad', 'jihad'. In his speeches, he commends the suicide bombers and glorifies their actions. When the notorious master terrorist Muhammad Abbas died in Iraq on 9 March 2004, Arafat was quick to issue a statement hailing his deeds:

"President Yasser Arafat, the Palestinian leadership, the Palestinian Liberation Organisation and the Palestinian National Authority, mourn the martyr leader Abu al-Abbas....The Palestinian leadership mourns him as a distinguished fighter and a national leader who devoted his life to serve his own people and his homeland".

Recall that among his many atrocities, Abu al-Abbas masterminded the hijacking of the cruise ship 'Achille Lauro' in 1985 and was responsible for the killing of an elderly disabled American Jewish tourist and dumping his body, together with his wheel chair, overboard. He had been wanted by the Americans, but moved to Iraq in 1986, where he was given sanctuary by Saddam Hussein. In April 2003, Abbas was captured by the Americans in Iraq and later died of heart attack while in custody.

Arafat's dream is to establish "an indivisible' Palestinian state from 'the sea to the river", even if the Palestinians have to "wait 100 years". He stubbornly refuses to disarm the terrorist organisations, holding them as a gun pointed at Israel's head. It is quite clear that as long as Arafat stays as the leader of the

Palestinians, the chances for peace will remain slim, and as long as terror is used as a political strategy, it will be difficult to envisage any solution to the Israeli Palestinian problem.

Arafat is not going to change, and if he stays the leader of the Palestinian people, instilling in them the hope of destroying Israel, things will not change. But, they can change if another trustworthy leader would take over from Arafat and lead his people to the path of peace and coexistence with Israel. If such a leader succeeded in bringing to a halt the terror and reversing the vitriolic preaching against the Jews and the Jewish state, it is certain that the Palestinians would achieve much better terms than they would ever achieve by violence and hatred. Yitzhaq Yefet was among the Israeli paratroopers who captured the old city of Jerusalem and was first to arrive at the Wailing Wall in 1967. He recently said: *"I used to want it to remain in our control for ever, but if it means real peace, not just on paper, we should give them the whole temple Mount".*[54] In the present situation this may sound heretic to many Israelis, but I believe that the majority would nevertheless agree to it, if they are convinced of real peace; not the one Arafat pretended to offer. When the late Egyptian President, Sadat, surprised the world by visiting Israel, he firstly declared that the Yom Kippur War was the last war between the two nations. *"There will be no war again"*, said Sadat, and *"all our differences will be solved by peaceful negotiations".* The final result was that the Israelis handed back to him all the Egyptian land captured in the Six-Day War.

On 4 March 2004 the Egyptian Government daily, al-Ahram, published an open letter from the veteran Egyptian author and columnist Anis Mansour, to Arafat. Mansour urged Arafat to submit to the counsel of the late President Sadat. He wrote:

"Listen to the words of those with more experience, wiser judgement, and clearer vision [than you]. This counsel is that you, or whoever represents you, sit [and negotiate] and raise the [Palestinian] demands before the eyes of the entire world. You and the entire world know that Sadat and Begin [the former Israeli Prime Minister] adopted a very similar principle—the honourable international custom of 'anything is negotiable'. You must negotiate so that you may refuse and agree...Now you know more than anyone else how many opportunities the Palestinian people have missed because of you. This is not my business, but it is your business and the business of your people, who sooner or later will call you to account...In light of what is currently happening, you understand how bloody the future [of the Palestinian people] is likely to be: There will be a total annihilation of the resources of the Palestinian people".

But Arafat is no Sadat. Arafat is devious, manipulative and untrustworthy. He had already negotiated in Camp David, but with narrow mindedness and lack of good faith. By contrast, Sadat was a man of vision and a man of his word, evoking trust and confidence. When shall such a 'Sadat' rise from the Palestinian people?

23

THE HOPE FOR PEACE

Golda Meir, an ex-prime minister of Israel, once said: *"peace will come when the Arabs start to love their children more than they hate us"*. On the 14th of January 2004 the first Hamas woman suicide bomber, Reem al-Reyashi, killed 4 Israelis and injured another 7. She was only 22 years old, a mother of two—a son of three and a one-year-old daughter. She committed her atrocious action at a border crossing where 6,000 Palestinians were seeking permits to work inside Israel. Perhaps she would not have succeeded in her crime had she not cried and pretended to be ill, faking a limp in order to be allowed to bypass the metal detectors, a callous and wicked exploitation of the humanitarian process, to say the least. In a farewell video film taken before her suicide bombing, she said that she hated the Zionists, loved her children, and that she did it in order to go to Paradise. Clearly, she hated the Jews more than she loved her children. Four Israeli young soldiers, who allowed her to bypass the metallic detector paid with their lives for being considerate. Other innocent losers will no doubt be the genuinely disabled Palestinians, who will pay the price at similar check posts in the future. There was also a distressing conclusion to this atrocity: the refusal of the Palestinian Prime Minister, Ahmed Qureia, to condemn the suicide attack, and the erection of a marquee for the guests who came to congratulate Reem's parents on her 'martyrdom', and to extol her 'heroic' action. I think it is such deeds, perhaps even more than the suicide bombing itself, which put away the prospect of peace.

We have already elaborated on the various obstacles for peace, which, in fact, could be condensed into one main cause, i.e. the Palestinian denial of Israel's right to exist and their hope of destroying it. The terror is the means, and the 'right of return' is the ploy used by the Palestinians to achieve this aim. I do not accept that settlements, or land, are the obstacle. The Arabs do not lack land and the Palestinians make up the majority of the population in Jordan, which, de facto, has already become a Palestinian state. Also, had the 'occupation' been the cause, the Palestinians would have not rejected Barak's offer in Camp David.

The question is whether, in spite of this dismal obstacle, peace is still achievable? The simple answer is that it is, if the main obstacle is removed. Arafat has been, and still is, that obstacle. He, as chairman of the Palestinian Authority, is the one responsible for the policy of hatred, terrorism and the instilment of the hope of destroying Israel into his people's minds. Not only the United States, but also the European Union has now tacitly recognized the deceitful and reckless character of Arafat. After so many years of autocracy, it is time the Palestinian people should ask what Arafat has achieved for them so far. Where is he leading them to? Who is responsible for the failures, setbacks and corruption? It is imperative for the sake of peace that a new, enlightened leader, takes over. A trustworthy leader who believes in a peaceful solution and recognizes Israel's right to exist as a Jewish state. A leader who is dedicated to democracy, prepared to reform the Palestinian Authority, outlaws the terrorist organisations, encourages the various movements to convert to political parties and consolidates all the various militant forces under one disciplined security authority. Such a change can be brought about if the Europeans join forces with the Americans, rather than go against them, as they have persistently been doing in recent years. The Europeans contribute about 60% of the total donations to the Palestinians, they are aware of the corruption and misuse of billions of dollar-donations by Arafat and his cronies, and they have strong influence on the Palestinians, if they would only decide to use it. But unfortunately rather than being helpful, they behave irresponsibly. They admit that Hamas is a terrorist organization, but, hypocritically, condemn Israel's targeting of Hamas' notorious terrorist leaders, dubbing it 'unlawful', in contrast to international law experts' opinion.[60] They know that Arafat is the obstruction for peace, but they still esteem him, instead of ostracizing him as the Americans have done. Even after Arafat had ousted the newly elected Palestinian Prime Minister Abu Mazen, who had the qualities and conviction to achieve peace, they made a minor, insignificant protest and soon returned to 'courting' Arafat.

Terrorism is not only Israel's scourge. The Europeans should recognize that if a democracy like Israel should cow to suicide bombing and terror, not only would Israel suffer a mortal danger, but also the Western Society, together with its democracy, freedom and values would be undermined. In the 60s and 70s of the last century, Palestinian terror against Israel was rampant, but the Europeans did not lift a finger against it. Even when it occurred against Israeli interests on European territory, they stood by and watched, and when terrorists, such as Lila Khalid and Muhammad Abbas fell into their hands, they freed them, believing it was only the fate of Israelis and Jews, and as long as they kept their distance, they were safe. This was a grave mistake and a lesson that took them long to learn. Only now have the Europeans awakened, when Europe has become the main focus and target of Islamist terrorism. But, they do not yet seem to realize that terrorism is terrorism, regardless of its causes and aims. They watch terrorists mutilate American civilians and suffice with empty words of support. The Europeans would do well, as long as it is still possible, to join the Americans and the Israelis in fighting terrorism everywhere with all their might, for if they do not, Islamic terrorism would eventually dictate to them how to behave and what to do. With Spain announcing their decision to withdraw their forces from Iraq, the terrorists have already scored a great victory, and the beginning of Western capitulation to terrorism may have already started.

The eradication of terror and the dismantling of the terrorist groups is one of the first prerequisites for real peace between Israel and the Palestinians. In fact it is also the first requirement of the 'Road Map', laid down by the United States, the European Union, Russia and the United Nations. The Palestinian Authority has the force, but not the will, to eradicate terror. A joint pressure and aid by the two powers can 'convince' them to do that. The eradication of Palestinian terrorism would become easier if the support and supplies given to them by certain countries were cut off. Terrorist groups depend on basic facilities, such as a base ('al-Qaida' means 'Base'), support, weapons, and funding, which are mainly being provided to them by Syria and Iran. Syria harbours, supports and trains several Palestinian terrorist organizations in Lebanon, while Iran supports and supplies Hamas and Hizbullah with weapons and harbours al-Qaida terrorists. Both countries turn a blind eye or rather give their blessing to al-Qaida terrorists who infiltrate Iraq from their territory, to stir instability and cause mayhem, chaos and panic. The sponsors of the 'Road Map', mainly the European Union and the United States, can change the attitude of such countries by using their economic and military might. They had already used diplomatic means which failed, they should now seriously warn such countries that if they did not heed to reason they would be severely punished, and the punishment would be so painful as to make their support for terrorism totally unworthy. On the 4th of March 2004, Tony Blair, the British Prime Minister, called for a change in international law to legitimise pre-emptive military action against rogue states, such as those that co-operated with terrorists. He added that Islamic extremism and terrorism posed a serious threat to the world and that it was time to rethink the old rule that limited armed intervention only to *"self defence in response to aggression"*. This seems to be the only way to deter rogue countries and defeat terrorism, but of course the declaration has to be translated into action first.

If the terrorist groups were disarmed and terrorism were brought to halt, Palestinian reform will be proved to be working; and if the Palestinian leadership denounced the 'further goal' of destroying Israel, then it is certain that Israel would respond most positively and would make, as its Prime Minister Sharon has already said, "painful compromises". Such reforms do not have to be concluded in order to alleviate Israel's concerns, they only have to be seriously declared and started, with a sincere aim to see them through. That would be enough to trigger a change of attitude and atmosphere for true peace.

In response to the first positive moves by the Palestinians, the Israelis should immediately start dismantling the settlements and withdrawing their forces to a line close to the 1967 border, in order to start the final peace discussions regarding any necessary border modifications. The land occupied by certain heavily populated settlements, such as Ma'ale Adumim and Ariel, for example, would be difficult, if not impossible, to dismantle and should be exchanged with other Israeli land, heavily populated with Israeli Arabs, such as Baka'a al-Gharbia and Um-al-Faham, notwithstanding the UN Resolution 242, which calls for the return of 'territories' and not 'all' the territories captured in 1967. As to Jerusalem, Clinton's proposal, which was agreed to by Barak, seems to be the most reasonable and just solution: *"everything Arab to the Palestinians and everything Jewish to the Israelis"*.

Both sides should make compromises. Israel should withdraw from the Gaza strip and the West Bank, the emotional heartland of their birthplace, and the Israelis should get assurances that their withdrawal would mean the end of the conflict. The Palestinians should abandon their unattainable demand for the "right of return" [al-Awda], which literally means the annihilation of Israel. The Palestinian refugees' plight is not to be blamed on Israel who accepted the United Nations' partition resolution in 1947, but on the Palestinians and the Arab countries that rejected it, invaded the newborn state and threatened to throw the Jews into the sea. After Israel's War of Independence in 1948, Jews were expelled from Arab countries and their property confiscated. Out of the 850,000 Arab Jews who had left their homes, about 600,000 of them flowed into Israel as refugees; they were all absorbed, and have been living in dignity ever since. The Palestinian and Jewish refugees can be considered as a population exchange, and it will not be the only one to have taken place in history. There had been many population exchanges in the past, suffice it to mention those between Turkey and Bulgaria, Turkey and Greece and India and Pakistan. The Jewish refugees were also not the only ones who had been absorbed and resettled in other countries. Before and after the Second World War about one hundred million people were displaced from their homes, all of whom were resettled in other countries and have lived happily in their new homes.

The only countries that have persistently refused to help or absorb their own refugees were the Arab states. There are 21 such states, with vast land expanses that total approximately 5.3 million square miles, compared with Israel's 8110 square miles, which amounts to only 0.15% of the Arab lands. The Arabs, therefore, do not lack land, and the problem could not have been about land. One asks: why would Palestinian refugees want to go back to their homes, which mostly do not exist anymore, in a country of different religion, language and culture and which they so much hate? The only plausible answer is their leaders' intention to overwhelm Israel and cause its collapse as a Jewish state. The real problem is therefore not the refugees, for had the Arab countries been concerned about the plight of their 'brethren', as they claimed, they would not have kept them in squalor and humiliation for over 55 years. The Arab states treated their Palestinian 'brethren' with contempt and callousness, using them as a political tool against Israel. In 1958, Ralph Galloway, UNRWA's (United Nations Relief and Work Agency) director, said: *"The Arab states do not want to solve the refugee problem. They want to keep it as an open sore and a weapon against Israel. Arab leaders do not give a damn whether the refugees live or die".*[28] The Arab states should now set right the wrong they had done and help the resettling of the Palestinian refugees in their vast countries and in the future Palestinian state. The refugees should be compensated for their loss of property by international funds. In fact, a sum of 15 billion dollars was suggested during the Camp David negotiations; an ample amount by any measure. The Jewish refugees, who were expelled from the Arab countries and left behind their homes and property, should not be forgotten when the Palestinian refugee issue is considered.

In the event of a peace agreement and the withdrawal of Israel to agreed borders, arrangements should be made to maintain its security, for a signed agreement in itself is not a guarantee for peace. The new Palestinian state should therefore be demilitarized and the Jordan valley, the new Palestinian eastern border, should be reconnoitred and patrolled by joint Israeli-Palestinian troops (UN Surveyors proved to be unreliable in such tasks), in order to prevent any breach of the agreement, or access of hostile Arab forces that may endanger the peace. Israel should, in any case, always maintain its military edge over its neighbours, for this would be the most effective assurance for peace.

To maintain the peace, the new Palestinian state should undertake to severely punish, not only those who commit acts of terror, but also those who preach or encourage terrorism. They should stop hatred and incitement against Israel and Jews and purge their entire education system, from the kindergartens and schools to the summer camps and the universities, instilling a new spirit of reconciliation and coexistence. They should purge their Press, Radio, TV, textbooks, computer games, Internet propaganda and religious sermons of hatred. Their spiritual leaders, who encourage suicide bombing by calling it "the highest degree of martyrdom", should be brought to justice on charge of incitement.

The intervention of the United States and the European Union would be needed for a considerable time after the peace accord. They should monitor the behaviour of both sides and the end of hatred and violence by the Palestinians, which should be prohibited by the terms and spirit of the agreement. The two 'Powers' should also monitor the Palestinian text books to ensure that there is no return to the old ways. In addition, they should control the monetary aid, which would flow into Palestine in order to alleviate poverty, create jobs and boost the economy; they should see to it that it is not spent on weapons or siphoned into private pockets. If this hope for the future is to materialise, then it would also be imperative to restrain the radical Muslim states, particularly Iran and Syria, who support and fund terrorism. This task can be achieved through a joint effort by the Americans and the Europeans, using a 'carrot and stick' policy, which, after the fall of Sadam Hussein, proved to be efficient in the case of Libya, which recently made a surprising turnaround, announcing its decision to abandon its efforts to develop weapons of mass destruction, and was embraced by the civilized world.

As the peace process starts to take effect, trust prevails between the parties, the general atmosphere being one of security, Israel should gradually dismantle the anti-terrorist fence, which was erected in order to protect its citizens against suicide bombers. Israel's 'belly' is very soft and only 9 miles wide at its narrowest location. Suicide bombers could cross freely from their bases into Israeli towns, often in just 5 to 15 minutes, and the only way to stop them is by erecting a fence, as proved successful in the Gaza Strip. The Palestinians complain about the fence and the check-points, but they have turned the whole of Israel into one big check-point; every school, every theatre, every coffee shop, every restaurant and every house-front in Israel have become a check-point. Living in peaceful coexistence, there is no need for check-points or fences between neighbours, as there is no fence or partition between Holland and Belgium, or Norway and Sweden. It should therefore be dismantled as soon as the reason for its original erection has been removed, although this may take some time, depending on the Palestinians, until confidence has been established.

If such changes would only start with a true intention, a beam of hope would gleam on the Holy Land, illuminating the path of peace and the future road to welfare and prosperity for both peoples. The Israelis, in their own interest, should extend every possible help and cooperation in developing the new Palestinian state, for they would be better off with a rich and prosperous neighbour, than with a poor one. In a secure and peaceful atmosphere, normal economic, industrial, technological, agricultural and cultural relations will develop to the benefit of both sides. The two peoples will come closer together and reap the harvest of peace and co-operation. I can see in my vision businesses, factories and projects managed by Palestinians and Israelis as equal partners. I can see in my vision Palestinian students from Bir-Zeit University qualifying for higher degrees in Israeli universities, and Jewish students studying Oriental sciences in the colleges of Palestine. I can also see Arab and Jewish children in common playgrounds, playing and chatting in two languages, and all Palestinians and Israelis living side by side, in peace and amity. And, in the words of the prophet: *"they shall beat their swords into ploughshares and their spears into pruning hooks; nation shall not lift up a sword against nation, neither shall they learn war anymore. But, they shall sit every man under his vine and under his fig tree, and none shall make them afraid".*

This is my dream for a just and lasting peace between the Israelis and the Palestinians, and although it is but a dream, a dream can sometimes come true, and this one must.

24

CONCLUSION

At the time of writing these lines however, in April 2004, Arafat is very much still at the Palestinian helm, running the show and determining the policy from his half demolished compound in Ramalla. After some pressure had been applied on him by the Americans and the Europeans he agreed to delegate some of his unlimited power to a Prime Minister. Abu Mazen, a moderate Palestinian leader who condemned violence and terrorism, was elected. He promised to disarm the terrorist organisations and was received with great enthusiasm by the Israelis and the Americans. He met with the Israeli Prime Minister in an amicable atmosphere, and was soon invited to the White House and was received with great honour and hospitality by President Bush. But Arafat did not seem to accept the idea that someone else was running the show, in contradiction to his policy. He did everything in his power to make Abu Mazen's position unsustainable. Abu Mazen was eventually forced to resign and Arafat regained power and full control, including that of the 'policing' forces. Subsequently, under additional pressure, Arafat appointed a new candidate. His choice fell on his long-time and loyal colleague, Ahmed Qureia (known as Abu Ala). In the short period since Abu Ala resumed the office of prime minister he has proven to be subservient to Arafat, consulting him on every issue and complying with his dictates.

Abu Ala has already formed his cabinet, but announced that he had no intention to disarm the terrorist organisations, which, as mentioned already, is the first and foremost requirement of the 'Road Map' and without which it is difficult to envisage the start of a serious peace process. Instead, he has been trying to convince Hamas to agree to a 'hudna' (ceasefire), but so far to no avail. The Israelis stated that they do no agreements with terrorists. They have, however, invited Abu Ala for peace talks, which he declined unless some concessions were made before hand.

Terrorism has not brought the Palestinian nearer to their aim. The contrary is true. President Bush has recently spoken to this effect, endorsing Sharon's plan to pull out from the Gaza Strip and maintain a few settlements in the West Bank. It was a clear signal to the Palestinians that they have failed to fight terrorism. It was a clear signal that time does not stand still; it goes by, bringing with it new realities that cannot be reversed, and what was achieved yesterday with Barak might be unachievable today with Sharon. It was a clear signal to the Palestinians to change their leadership, their policy of terror and their persistent rejectionism. But, instead, Arafat responded by reiterating his hackneyed demand of the "right of return", which he—as well as the whole world—knows that it is unattainable.

Consequently, the situation is tense at the moment, and a 'miracle' is needed to pull out the peace wagon from the quagmire, but as Ben-Gurion once said: *"In Israel, to be realistic, one has to believe in miracles"*. There are nevertheless a few encouraging signs of hope on the horizon. Both sides, especially the Palestinians, have had more than their share of suffering and seem to be exhausted by the incessant conflict. There has been the 'Geneva Initiative', instigated and signed by prominent, though unauthorised, leaders of Israel and the PLO, which is a heartening omen of willingness and yearning for peace by both sides. Also, the Europeans, as well as the Americans, expressed their confidence that the pull out from the Gaza Strip would open a new avenue to reviving the Road Map. Arafat has been isolated for a long time and his international status has plummeted; he is in his late seventies and it is quite reasonable to assume that he will eventually be replaced, and not in the remote future, by a younger and more pragmatic and flexible leader. Sharon is also in his seventies, but despite the vilification of him, he is needed for peace, for he is the kind of leader who can make 'painful compromises' and still be trusted by most Israelis. Also, after the defeat of Sadam Hussein and the change of regime in Iraq, and after the recent surprising Libyan turnaround, it is quite possible that the heat would be turned up on Iran and Syria, who are the two fanatical countries in the region that stir Palestinian violence and support terrorism.

Things may seem gloomy at the moment, but in the Middle East the unexpected often happens. One unexpected event can change the course of history, create a new atmosphere, and the dream of peace would, against all odds, still come true.

Bibliography

1. The Hebrew People—Josephine Kamm — Victor Gollanz, London, 1967

2. The Jewish War—Josephus Flavius—translated by G.A. Williamson — Penguin Book, Harmondsworth, 1970

3. Masada—Yigael Yadin — Hebrew University, Jerusalem, 1989

4. Bar Kochba—Encyclopaedia Judaica — Peter publishing House, Jerusalem

5. Bar Kochba-Yigael Yadin — Weidenfeld & Nicolson, London, 1971

6. The Latin Kingdom of Jerusalem—Joshua Prawer — Weidenfeld & Nnicolson, London, 1972

7. Code Civil de Francais—Napoleon Bonapar — Reference Library of political ocuments, (Internet)

8. The Life and Times of Muhammad—John Glubb — Hodder & Stoughton, London, 1970

9. The Prophet Muhammed—Barnaby Rogerson — Little, Brown, London, 2003

10. Personal Witness—Abba Eban — G.P. Putnam's sons, New York, 1992

11. Supreme Command—Eliot A. Cohen — The Free Press, New York, 2002

12. Ben-Gurion—Michael Bar-Zohar (Hebrew) · Am Oved Publishers, Tel-Aviv, 1976

13. Holy Land Unholy War—Anton LaGuardia · John Murray Ltd, London, 2001

14. My War With Israel—King Hussein of Jordan

15. In My Way—Goerge Brown · Victor Gollancz, London, 1971

16. Harakiri—Raviv Druker (Hebrew) · Miskal, Yedioth Ahronoth, Tel-Aviv, 02

17. Imad al-Falouji at a symposium in Gaza · al-Ayyam (Palestinian daily), 6.12.00

18. Arafat addressing a popular delegation · Palestine News Agency, 01.12.2001

19. Arafat addressing a delegation from Hebron · Palestine Television, 26.01.2002

20. Arafat addressing thousands of Palestinians · Voice of Palestine Radio, 26.01.2002

21. Arafat speaking to a crowd of Palestinians · Palestine satellite TV Channel, 1.02.02

22. Palestinian politician in presence of Arafat · PalestineSatellite TV Channel, 1.01.02

23. Mustafa Najim, a priest preaching · Palestine Satellite TV Ch., 02.02.02

24. A document signed by Arafat, approving the Purchase of 250 Kalashnikovs to Tanzim · Published in December 2001

25. David Rivkin, Lee Casey and Darin Bartram, Partners in the Washington DC office of Baker & Hosteller LLP · Jerusalem Post, 7.11.2002

26. The Quran—translated by N. J. Dawood · Penguin Classics, London, 1990

27. The Holy Bible · Cambridge Univ. Press, Cam, 1989

28. From Time Immemorial—Joan Peters | JKAP Publications, USA, 2002

29. Israel and Palestine—Bernard Wesserstein | Profile books Ltd., New York, 2002

30. The Arabs in History—Bernard Lewis | Oxford Press, New York, 1993

31 The Crisis of Islam—Bernard Lewis | Phoenix, London, 1993

32. Living Islam—Akbar ahmed | BBC Books Ltd., London, 1993

33. A History of the bible | Phaidon Press ltd., London, 2001

34. Six Days of War—Michael Owen | Oxford university Press, London, 2001

35. Myths and Facts—Mitchel G. Bard | AICE—Chevy Chase MD, USA, 2002

36. Population and Development Review—P. Fargues | Population Council—September 2000

37. Intifada—Zeev Schiff & Ehud Yaari | Simon & Schuster, New York, 1989

38. Israel, a History—Martin Gilbert | Transworld Publishers, London, 1998

39. Righteous Victims—Zionist Arab Conflict—Benny Morris | John Murray Ltd., London, 2000

40. Muhammad—Karen Armstrong | Phoenix, London, 1993

41. A short History of the Arab People—John Glubb | Hodder & Stoughton, London, 1969

42. Progress Report of the United Nations Mediator on Palestine. | Third Session Supplement No.11 (a\648), Paris, 1948.

43. A History of The Jewish People—H. H. Ben Sasson | Harvard University Press, Boston, 1985

44. Intelligence and Terrorism Information Centre | Information Bulletin No.2, March, 02

45.	Information Internet Division	Ministry of Foreign Affairs, Jerusalem
46.	My Country—Abba Eban	Wieden and Nicolson, London, 1972
47.	Heritage—Abba Eban	Wieden and Nicolson, London, 1984
48.	The Innocents Abroad—Mark Twain	The American Publishing Co., 1899
49.	An Introduction to Islam—Fredrick M. Denny	Macmillan, Basingstoke, 1994
50.	Hadith Literature—Muhammad Z. Siiddiqi	Islamic Texts Society, Cam., 1993
51.	The Arab-Israel conflict (its history in maps)—Martin Gilbert	Weidenfeld and Nicolson, London, 79
52.	The Israel-Arab Reader—Walter Laqueur	Weidenfeld and Nicolson, London, 69
53.	Storm From The East—Robert Marshall	BBC, London, 1993
54.	Interview by the reporter Toby Harnden	The Daily Telegraph, 17 January 2004
55.	Interview by the reporter George Jones	The Daily Telegraph, 24 January 2004
56	The Quran—translated by N. J. Dawood	Penguin Group, N.Y, 1994
57	The Jews of the Sudan—Eli Malka	Syracuse University Press, N.Y., 1997
58	Palestine under the British—Tom Segev	Keter Publishing House, Jerusalem, 99

| 59 | The Case for Israel—Alan Dershowitz | John Wiley & Sons, Inc., 2003 |
| 60 | 'They don't have to wear combats to be a fair target'—Article by Alan Dershowitz | 'The Times'—London daily, Thursday 22 April 2004 (page 20). |

.

Index

A

Abbas, Muhammad 184, 190
Abbasids 63
Abdel Nasser, Gammal 91, 101, 102, 105, 106
Abdel-Rahman, Ahmad 163
Abraham 1, 2, 3, 40
Abram 1
Abu al-Abbas 47
Abu Bakr 46
Abu Talib 33
Abu-Arbiah, Othman 180
Abu-Mazen 198
Abu-Salam, Salim Alo'aida 180
Abu-Shamala, Fayad 161
Aelia Capitolina 20
Ahad Ha'am 52
Aisha 46
Aizenman, Pnina 136
Al-Ahram 185
Alami, Musa 176
Al-Aqsa 38, 136, 161, 177
Al-aqsa Martyrs 136, 147, 149
Albania 50
Al-Bukhari 38, 44
Al-Buraq 39, 62
Alexander the Great 13
Al-Falouji, Imad 132, 202

Al-Haram al-Sharif 63
Al-Hourani, Abdullah 179
al-Husseini, Haj Amin 67, 70, 85, 182
Al-Jabar 47
Al-Jami al-Sahih 38
Al-Kawukji, Fawzi 71
Al-Khawarizma 47
Allenby, Edmund 67
Al-Mahdi 61, 62
al-Masri, Majd 149
Almohades, Berber 26
Al-muwahidun 26
Al-Qaida 46, 140, 190, 191
al-Rashid, Harun 47
Al-Reyashi, Reem 139, 187
Anatolia 48, 50
Annan, Kofi 117, 159
Antiochus IV of Syria 13
Antipater 15
Anti-Semitism 51, 56, 57, 133, 150, 151, 163
Apes & Swines 43
Arab Revolt 71, 72, 78
Arabia 34, 58, 66, 67, 68, 100, 102, 140, 167
Arafat, Yasser 118, 121, 128, 136, 184

Arakat, Saeb 181
Arane, Ike 76
Arendt Hana 154
Ark of the Covenant 10
Aron, Raymond 154
Aryan languages 56
Aryan race 56
Aryan stock 56
Assaffah 47
Associated Press 161, 163, 164,
    165
Assyira 10, 11

B

Babylonia 11, 12, 15, 22, 32
Baghdad 47, 48, 49, 63
Baka'a al-Gharbia 192
Balfour Declaration 54, 66, 68, 73,
    175
Balfour, Arther James 53, 54, 69
Barak, Ehud 124, 134
Barak, Gudge 5
Barghouti, Marwan 149
Bar-Kochba, Simon 20
Basle, Switzerland 53
Bathsheba 9, 10
Battle of Bedr 36, 44
Battle of the Roads 86
Battle of Uhud 36
Begin, Menahem 75, 115
Belgium 31, 196
Ben-Ami, Shlomo 126, 130
Ben-Gurion, David 55
Ben-Mattetiahu, Joseph 16
Berber 26
Berlin, Isaiah 154
Bernstein, Leonard 154

Bethar 20, 22
Bible xiii, 1, 2, 3, 13, 15, 22, 23,
    32, 37, 73, 75, 182, 202, 203
Black Death 25, 49
Black Stone 34, 36
Blair, cherie 137
Blair, Tony 191
Blitz Krieg 49, 57
Blood Libel 24, 25, 150, 181
Blood Shedder 47
Bomberg, David 154
Bonaparte, Napoleon 28, 30
Brener, Chaim 70
British mandate 66, 67, 72, 78, 79
Buber, Martin 154
Bull, General Odd 103
Byzantine, Byzantium 50, 60

C

Caliphs 36, 41, 42, 46, 48
Camp David 125, 126, 127, 128,
    129, 130, 131, 132, 134, 135,
    174, 186, 188, 194
Canaan ix, xiii, 1, 2, 3, 4
Chagall, Marc 154
Chancellor, John 73
Charlemagne 23
Chart of Omar 45
Church of Nativity 166
Columbus, Christopher 27
Constantine, Roman Emperor 60
Constantinople 50, 60
Conversos 26, 27
Conversos, Spain 26
Converts 26
Cromwell, Oliver 28
Crusade, Crusaders 24, 63

Crystal Night 57
Cyrus, Persian King 12

D

Darwin, Charles 56
David, King of Israel 9, 10
Dayan, Moshe 75, 77, 97, 114
De Rothschild, Edmond 52
Deborah 5
Declaration of Independence 87, 88
Defensive Shield 156, 157, 158
Dershowitz, Alan 172, 205
Devil Island 51
Dir Yassin 92, 93, 94
Disraeli, Benjamin 28
Dome of the Rock 62, 63
Dreyfus, Alfred 51

E

Eban, Aba 76, 78, 88, 100, 129
Edumean 15
Egypt ix, 3, 9, 10, 11, 13, 26, 34, 46, 63, 89, 91, 96, 97, 98, 99, 100, 101, 102, 103, 104, 109, 113, 116, 134, 150, 151, 167, 179, 182, 183
Einstein, Albert 56
Eleazar Ben-Ya'eer 17
Elijah, prophet 40
Emir Faisal of Arabia 66, 67
Eshkol, Levi 101
Euphrates 1, 9, 11, 67, 152
Europeans 135, 146, 155, 189, 190, 195, 198, 200
Exodus 3, 11, 76, 79
Exodus from Egypt 11

Exodus, Refugee Ship 76
Ezra xii, 12, 13

F

Fedayeen 96
Final Solution 57, 85
Flavius Josephus 17
France 23, 24, 30, 31, 49, 56, 98, 99, 100, 102, 170
Freud, Lucien 154

G

Gabriel, angel 35, 39, 62
Galilee 15, 16, 17, 20, 28, 65
Galloway, Ralph 193
General Assembly, UN 58
General Syrian congress 66, 174
Genghis Khan 49
Germany 24, 31, 49, 51, 52, 53, 56, 57, 71, 76, 85, 150
Gertler, Mark 154
Gessius Florus 16
Gideon 5
Ginzberg, Asher 55
Gobineau, Joseph 56
Golan Heights 69, 101, 104, 111, 112
Goliath, Philistine 8
Gordon, Charles 61
Guy Mollet 98

H

Hadith 37, 38, 39, 40, 43, 44, 45, 46, 183, 204
Hadrian, Roman Emperor 19, 20
Hafsa, Muhammad's wife 46
Halevi, Jehuda 26

Hamas 44, 46, 145, 147, 162, 165, 171, 183, 187, 189, 191, 199
Hanukkah 14
Haran ix, 1, 2
Hashim 33
Hasmonaean Family 14
Haycraft Commission 70
Heavenly Rewards 42
Hebrew xii, 2, 12, 162, 201, 202
Hebron 2, 9, 64, 70, 71, 179, 202
Hefetz, Jascha 154
Helena 30, 31, 60
Herod 15, 18, 62
Herzl, Theodore 52
Hess, Moses 52
Hezbullah 117, 148
Hijra 35, 39, 43, 152
Hilel 15
Hitler, Adolf 153
Hizbullah 46, 136, 191
Holland 31, 196
Holy Sepulchre 48
Houris 42, 146
Hussein al-Sharif 68
Husseini, Faisal 179

I
Ibn Gabirol, Solomon 26
Ibn Nagrela, Samuel 26
Ibn Shaprut, Hasdai 26
Inquisition, Spain 27
Intifada xi, xiii, 117, 118, 130, 131, 132, 150, 157, 161, 166, 169, 177, 179, 203
Irgun Tsvai Leumi 75
Isaac 2, 3

Isaiah 10, 154
Ish-Bosheth 9
Islam xiii, 26, 33, 34, 36, 37, 38, 41, 42, 43, 46, 47, 48, 50, 61, 62, 63, 133, 138, 146, 182, 203, 204
Islamic Jihad 147
Israel ix, xii, xiii, 1, 3, 4, 5, 8, 9, 10, 11, 13, 32, 54, 55, 58, 60, 61, 62, 65, 66, 75, 77, 78, 85, 87, 89, 91, 93, 94, 96, 97, 98, 99, 100, 101, 102, 103, 104, 105, 106, 107, 109, 110, 111, 113, 114, 115, 116, 117, 118, 120, 121, 124, 125, 126, 127, 128, 129, 130, 131, 132, 133, 134, 135, 136, 137, 138, 139, 140, 141, 142, 143, 144, 145, 146, 147, 148, 149, 150, 152, 153, 156, 157, 158, 159, 161, 162, 164, 166, 167, 169, 170, 171, 172, 174, 177, 178, 179, 180, 181, 182, 183, 184, 185, 187, 188, 189, 190, 191, 192, 193, 194, 195, 196, 199, 200, 202, 203, 204, 205
Italy 27, 30
Izzidin al-Kasam 71

J
Jacob 2, 3, 4
Jaffa 70, 143, 179
Jarrar, Nasser 165
Jenin 89, 156, 158, 159, 163, 164, 165, 181
Jeremiah 10
Jericho 4, 15, 65, 120
Jerusalem xi, 9, 10, 11, 12, 13, 14, 15, 16, 17, 19, 20, 23, 24, 32, 35, 37, 38, 39, 40, 48, 52, 54,

60, 61, 62, 63, 64, 65, 67, 69, 70, 79, 85, 86, 88, 89, 90, 91, 92, 93, 103, 104, 124, 125, 136, 144, 162, 167, 170, 176, 177, 179, 180, 181, 182, 185, 192, 201, 202, 204
Jesus xii, 15, 23, 40, 60
Joseph 3, 4, 16, 27, 56
Josephus, Plavius 182
Joshua 4, 65, 201
Judah xiii, 4, 9, 10, 11, 13, 14, 15, 60
Judea xii, 14, 15, 16, 19, 20, 22, 55, 60, 131

K
Ka'aba 34, 36, 39
Kadoura, Musa 159
Kaffa 49
Kalischer, Zevi 52
Karina A, ship 147
Khadija, Muhammad's wife 35
Kharkov 31
Khartoum 61, 106, 109, 177
Kibbutz Tel-Hay 69
Kibya 97
King David Hotel 77
King Ferdinand 26
King Hussein 103, 105, 109, 115, 116, 202
King-Crane Commission 66, 174
Kitaj, R.B. 154
Kitchener, Horatio 62

L
Lazarus, Emma 29
League of nations 67, 68, 78
Lehi 76, 92, 93

Libermann, Max 154
Libya 195
Lion Heart, Richard 24
Lord Moyne 76
Lovers of Zion 52

M
Ma'ale Adumim 192
Maccabeans 14, 16, 60
MacMichael, Harold 73, 75
Mahler, Gustav 154
Maimonedes, Moses 26
Mamluks 48, 63
Mamre 2
Mandeel, Suleiman 62
Mansour, Anis 185
Marrih, Wilhelm 56
Masada 18, 201
McMahon, Henry 68
Mecca 33, 34, 35, 36, 37, 38, 39, 45, 63
Medina 35, 36, 43, 44, 45, 63, 152
Mendelssohn, Jakob Ludwig 154
Menuhin ,Yehudi 154
Miraj 40
Mishna 22
Mitchell Committee 132, 133
Modigliani, Amedeo 154
Mongols 48, 49, 50, 63
Montgomery, Bernard 72
Montifiore, Sir Moses 29
Moors, Muslims in Spain 25, 28
Moscow 31
Moses 3, 4, 12, 26, 29, 40, 52, 183
Mount Corpus 88, 93, 104
Mount Hira 35

Mount Uhud 36
Muawya 47
Muhammad 33, 34, 39, 41, 44,
    46, 142

N
Najim, Mustafa 146, 202
Napoleon 30
Nathan, prophet 9, 10
Nazi 49, 56, 76, 85, 133, 150
Nazi Propaganda 56, 133, 150
Nehemiah 12
Neron 16
Night Journey 37, 39, 62
Nobel Prize 154, 155

O
O'Meara, Dr. Barry 30
Old Testament xii, xiii, 44, 54, 182
Omer, Chaliph 46
Ottoman 50, 63, 182

P
PA 124, 162, 163
Palestine ix, xii, xiii, 20, 22, 23,
    24, 28, 32, 48, 52, 53, 54, 55,
    58, 60, 61, 62, 63, 64, 65, 66,
    67, 68, 69, 70, 71, 72, 73, 74,
    76, 77, 78, 79, 80, 85, 86, 87,
    88, 101, 102, 114, 120, 121,
    131, 143, 170, 174, 175, 176,
    179, 180, 182, 183, 195, 196,
    202, 203, 204
Palestinian Authority 120, 124,
    131, 132, 135, 142, 143, 147,
    162, 167, 178, 188, 190
Palestinian Refugees 126, 146,
    192, 193, 194
Park Hotel 156, 157

Peel, Royal Commission 72
People of the Book 35, 43, 45, 61
Perlman, Yitzhak 154
Persian Empire 46
Persians 12, 61
Philistia 19, 20, 60
Philistines 4, 5, 8, 9
Pinsker, Leo 52
Pissaro, Camille 154
Pogroms 25, 28, 32, 151
Pompey 14, 15
Population exchange 193
Portugal 27, 31
President Bush 198, 199
President Wilson 66
Prince Abdullah Hussein 68
Prince of the Believers 46
Promised Land 1, 3, 4, 52, 64, 183
Ptolemy 13
Purity of Arms 157

Q
Queen Isabella 26
Quraida, Jewish tribe 35, 45
Quran 33, 35, 36, 37, 38, 40, 42,
    43, 44, 45, 46, 142, 143, 146,
    182, 183, 202, 204
Quraysh 33
Qureia, Ahmed 187, 198

R
Rabbi Akiva 20
Ramalla 181, 198
Rantisi, Abdel-Aziz 145, 172
Refugees 76, 79, 92, 96, 126, 137,
    146, 178, 192, 193, 194
Right of Return 126, 188, 192, 199

Riots 66, 69, 70, 71, 72, 74, 134, 176
Romans 14, 15, 16, 17, 18, 20
Ross, Dennis 135
Rothschild, Edmond 52
Rubenstein, Artur 154
Russia 28, 29, 31, 32, 49, 52, 99, 100, 151, 190

S
Sabra 116
Sabri, Ikrima 179
Sadat, Anwar 109
Safed 28, 64
Saladin 26
Samaria 10, 11, 131, 149
Samson 5
Samuel, Herbert 73
Samuel, prophet 4
Sanjaks 64
Saqer, Turki Muhammad 152
Saragon II 10
Saul, King of Israel 8
Schoenberg, Arnold 154
Seamen, Daniel 162
Security Fence 139, 140, 167
Security zone 117, 124, 136, 137
Seleucids 13
Seljuks 48, 63
September 11 138, 163, 164, 173
Settlements 52, 55, 58, 65, 66, 70, 71, 78, 86, 116, 119, 123, 143, 146, 174, 188, 192, 199
Severus, Julius 20
Shaath, Nabil 166
Shaheeds 133, 143, 144, 146, 148
Shahian, Abdel-Aziz 178

Shahin, Seif El Din 162
Shammai 15
Sharia 41
Sharon, Ariel 97, 111, 117, 130, 132
Shatilla 116
Shehadeh, Salah 171
Shia'as 39, 42, 48
Shiites 41
Shubaki, Fuad 148
Sisera 5
Solomon, King of Israel 10
Soutine, Chaim 154
Spain 10, 23, 25, 26, 27, 28, 31, 47, 49, 61, 190
Special Night Squads 74
Spinoza, Barukh 154
Spiritual Zionism 55
St Helena 30
Struma, ship 76
Subedei, Mongol General 49
Suez Canal 91, 98, 101, 104, 109, 111, 112
Suleiman the magnificent 50
Sunnan 38
Sunnis 39, 41, 42
Synagogues 28, 32, 45, 69, 71
Syria ix, 13, 14, 16, 34, 46, 47, 48, 61, 64, 66, 67, 69, 71, 77, 96, 97, 100, 101, 102, 103, 109, 113, 124, 134, 153, 167, 174, 175, 176, 182, 190, 195, 200

T
Taggart, Charles 72
Talmud xii, 22, 23, 28, 181
Tanzim, Militia 147, 149

Targeting of terrorists 166, 170
Temple Mount 62, 125, 126, 127,
    130, 131, 132, 164, 177, 182,
    185
Temujin, Ginghis Chan 49
Terrorism 46, 119, 120, 123, 124,
    133, 134, 135, 138, 139, 141,
    144, 147, 153, 158, 159, 169,
    170, 178, 188, 189, 190, 191,
    194, 195, 198, 199, 200, 203
The Golden Age 26
The Hagana 71, 73, 74, 75, 77,
    78, 86, 87, 89
The Jewish State 52, 54, 58, 72,
    79, 86, 87, 88, 89, 106, 129,
    136, 180, 183, 185
The Media xi, 113, 150, 159, 161,
    163, 166, 167, 181
The Temple 12, 14, 15, 16, 17,
    19, 20, 32, 60, 62, 125, 126,
    130, 131, 132, 164, 177, 182
The Twelve tribes 4, 10
Tiberias 64
Tiran straits 97, 98, 99, 101, 102
Titus 16, 17, 32, 38, 60
Togrul Beg 48
Tongue, Jenny 137
Torah 3, 12, 13, 14
Trajan, Emperor 19
Trans-jordan 68, 69
Tribe of Ukl 44
Turkmans 48
Twain, Mark 64, 204

U
Um al-Faham 192
Umayyad 47, 63
UN General Assembly 58

UN Resolution 181 80
UN Resolution 242 192
United nations 78, 79, 80, 87,
    100, 105, 106, 117, 120, 159,
    176, 190, 192, 193, 194, 203
United States 29, 32, 98, 99, 100,
    110, 111, 172, 188, 190, 191,
    195
UNRWA 193
Ur ix, 1
Urban II, Pope 23
Uriah 9
Uthman 46, 47

V
Vengerov, Maxim 154
Vespasian 16, 17

W
Wailling Wall 17
Waterloo 31
Wauchope, Arther 73
Weizmann, Chaim 53, 175
Weizmann, Ezer 91
West Bank 66, 91, 92, 104, 109,
    111, 112, 113, 114, 118, 119,
    131, 134, 135, 139, 163, 165,
    172, 174, 177, 182, 192, 199
White Paper 73, 74, 75, 77, 78
Wingate, Charles 74
World War I 68, 71
World War II 71

Y
Yadin, Yigael 18, 21
Yathrib 35
Yefet, Yitzhak 185
Yehiyeh, Abdel-Razik 148

Yellow Badge 45
Yigael Alon 75
Yodpat 16
Yodpat (Jotapata) 16
York 24, 29, 164, 201, 203
Young Turks 66

Z
Zion 9, 52, 54, 151, 153
Zionism xiii, 51, 52, 53, 54, 55, 58, 142, 176
Zukerman, Pinhas 154

0-595-32133-X

Printed in the United Kingdom
by Lightning Source UK Ltd.
101304UKS00002B/67-255